THERE IS NO A.I.

A Scientific Exploration

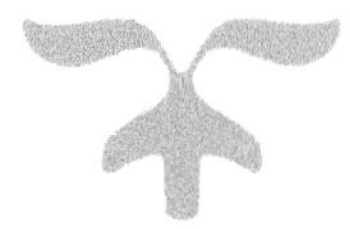

There Is No A.I.

There Is No A.I.

There Is No A.I.

Contents

Acknowledgement

This book would not have been possible without countless discussions with my mentor, Mr. Rupam Das, who has always guided me in the pursuit of knowledge. I have been fortunate enough to be blessed by different gurus at different junctures of life, especially when I have been seeking an answer to a question with all my sincerity. Mr Rama Seshan Chandrasekharan is one such divine personality, with immense knowledge on various subjects, who has generously spent a lot of his valuable time to explain to me different aspects of philosophy and literature. Much of the context in this book has been derived from various conversations I have had in the recent past with friends as well as strangers, trying to understand their perspective on the subject of *"Artificial Intelligence"*.

To pursue a project, such as writing a book, takes a lot of effort and discipline, but also concentration. My boss, Mr Ashish Agarwal, has thoroughly helped in my career at Eversana by making sure I am not overburdened with unnecessary tasks and have ample time to pursue my creative interests.

This journey would have never been complete without the support of my lifelines, Richa and Maithili. *I love you both, and you complete me*!

Preface

"The ultimate measure of a man is not where he stands in moments of comfort, but where he stands at times of challenge and controversy. ~ Martin Luther King Jr."

The words we choose to convey our thoughts are of utmost importance, and I am guilty of writing a book titled `Objects, data & A.I.` without fully grasping the meaning of the word `intelligence`. I was a novice back in 2023 and a student still, but 2 years is a long duration to make one realize the mistakes committed in the past. And what good is a man if he cannot claim responsibility for the actions committed and stand for correcting them when the realization occurs.

But why this sudden realization?

Plato said, *"The worst of all deceptions is self-deception"*. No realization is sudden. Our brain is designed by the Creator to denounce the lies, no matter how rewarding we may find them. One may be attracted to the false idols, and everything may seem to fall in place perfectly at the beginning, yet the brain starts rejecting the lie within. Now, one may choose to live the lie and not face the sword, but cowardice is not the act of a man!

In the fall of 2024, I was re-watching the movie Fight Club, and there was a particular monologue by Brad Pitt's character that struck me. Tyler Durden (Pitt's character in the movie) remarks, *"Advertising has us chasing cars and clothes, working jobs we hate, so we can buy shit we don't need "*.

There Is No A.I.

Of late, there have been a lot of headlines covering the fall of the IT industry and the layoff of *humans*. A certain narrative is being built that humans are easily replaceable. CEOs of tech giants like Meta, Microsoft, etc. have been constantly saying to each other on a global platform that in the coming years, there won't be any need for humans to code. The AI models have far exceeded humans in the level of intelligence! A sense of fear has gripped the hearts of computer scientists ever since the parading of Large Language Models had started in mainstream media, portraying it as the next epoch of human revolution.

But for reasons unknown, my brain has not been able to digest this idea. When a product is a genuine innovation that is meant to solve a specific problem, it organically finds its foothold. However, when a darker agenda needs to be planted in society, stories and narratives are woven accordingly.

A product may seem to you a non-living entity, but do keep in mind it resembles the thought process of its creator, thus the genes. There is a reason why Hitler could only promote anarchy, and Einstein proposed relativity. There is a reason why philosophy has been systematically eliminated from education, so that hedonism can be promoted. Remember the line from The Lord of the Rings: *"One ring to rule them all"*.

So yes, A.I. has to be a one-stop solution for everything! And the very humans who have built this `so-called` mega technology stand no chance.

Yet, I refuse to believe that. I refuse to believe that the heads of capitalism can truly build a model that resembles human intelligence. However, I bet on them to parade whatever they have built as the next big thing. After all, what can be a better way to sell something that is not even required in most fundamental scenarios? Moreover, if you convince a herd that they are of no importance and can easily be replaced, and when the spirit within them dies, they surrender to the whims of capitalists to cling to any hope of survival.

In his essays, Steve Biko often used the phrase, *"The most potent weapon in the hands of the oppressor is the mind of the oppressed"*. But how do you free such an oppressed mind in the first place?

Genevan philosopher Jean-Jacques Rousseau argues that a man is not born free, but everywhere he is in chains. These chains are made of social conventions, inequality, unjust institutions, and systems of control that limit his freedom not by necessity, but by artificial design. However, Rousseau does not despair for mankind's miserable condition but calls for reform. He writes in Book I of *Émile*, *"We are born weak, we need strength; we are born unprovided, we need aid; we are born stupid, we need judgment. All that we lack at birth, all that we need when we come to man's estate, is the gift of education"*.

So, the path of knowledge be it! Knowledge never consists in a manipulation of man and nature as opposite forces or in the reduction of data to mere statistical order but is a means of liberating mankind from the destructive power of fear, pointing the way toward the goal of the rehabilitation of the human will and the rebirth of faith and confidence in the human person.

There Is No A.I.

In my quest to restore faith in the human brain, I had to understand its intricacies, and at the same time, I had to expose the limitations of its threat, i.e., Artificial Intelligence, *aka A.I.,* which is poised to replace the human workforce. I took a scientific approach. Rather than believing what is being fed on my timeline about the capabilities of A.I. models, I started to dive into the functioning of the human brain and meditate upon its mathematical modelling, and compare it with the functioning of A.I. models. And now I am sharing with you whatever I have learnt so far in this eye-opening expedition.

By no means am I claiming that I understand this unique piece of creation by the Creator himself, for many have long treaded this curious path before me and yet have remained amazed by its mysteries. I, being a novice in this journey, am just holding on to the observation presented by the greats in the field of neuroscience and mathematics. And if I have to be brutally honest here, then all I am doing is collating whatever I discovered and presenting it to you to ignite your quests.

"Ignorance is the night of the mind, but a night without moon or star." ~ Confucius.

There Is No A.I.

There Is No A.I.

There Is No A.I.

AI: Understanding Current Landscape

In science, it is not speed that is the most important. It is the dedication, the commitment, the interest, and the will to know something and to understand it - these are the things that come first. - Eugene Wigner

In the ancient Indian debate system, there is a tradition of engaging the *other* using a technique called *'pūrvapakṣa'*, where one must first study the *other's* viewpoint very seriously and then only can debate against it. It may even be regarded as the *prima facie* view on a subject, often established as a point of debate within philosophical discourse. Continuing with the tradition of the land where I belong, I must lay before you the foundational architecture of the current models of Machine Learning, which are being called A.I., *aka* `Artificial Intelligence`.

Disclaimer: By no means and in no capacity, I intend to degrade the decades of effort which has been poured into building these models. Honestly speaking, they are a work of art, science, and mathematics, the foundations of which were laid by some very creative and visionary human minds like Warren McCulloch, Walter Pitts, Alan Turing, Frank Rosenblatt, Geoffrey Hinton, Ian Goodfellow, and others. My discourse lies with the usage of the word *'Intelligence'* by the tech proprietors to demean the uniqueness of human intelligence and its creative capabilities, which even the great minds, who shaped this field of study, did not ever implied. We shall, however, go into this debate at a later stage.

Galileo Galilei famously wrote: *"Philosophy is written in this grand book, the universe, which stands continually open to our gaze. But the book cannot be understood unless one first learns to comprehend the language and read the letters in which it is composed. It is written in the language of mathematics, and its characters are triangles, circles, and other geometric figures without which it is humanly impossible to understand a single word of it; without these, one wanders about in a dark labyrinth".*

Historically, this question has been asked many times: *Isn't science quite independent of philosophy?* Many even believe that modern science has become effective by dropping philosophy. Newton's Mathematical Principles of Natural Philosophy (1687) emphasized deriving laws from observations. His physics was seen as a triumph of empirical science. He presented his work as grounded in empirical observations, which avoided speculative hypotheses about unobservable causes. However, if his theories were purely derived from facts, they would be as certain and unchangeable as the data itself. Let us inspect.

Newton's laws of motion and universal gravitation described the behavior of physical objects in a framework of absolute space and absolute time. Space was considered a fixed, unchanging stage, and time flowed uniformly, independent of any physical process. When James Clerk Maxwell's equations unified electricity and magnetism, they established that light is an electromagnetic wave. But it raised a critical question: *"If light is a wave, what medium does it travel through?"*.

In classical wave mechanics, waves require a medium; for example, sound travels through air, and water waves travel through water. Hence, physicists hypothesized a medium for light, the *luminiferous ether* (from Latin, meaning "light-bearing ether"). The ether was imagined as an invisible, all-pervading, and stationary medium that filled the universe, serving as the medium through which electromagnetic waves, including light, propagated. It was assumed to be weightless, transparent, and frictionless, yet rigid enough to support the high-speed oscillations of light waves. Hinging on the *'ether'* theory, scientists predicted that the Earth's orbital velocity would produce a relative motion against the stationary ether, which in turn would alter the speed of light measured in different directions. For example, to an observer, light traveling parallel to the Earth's motion would face a "headwind", slowing its effective speed, while light traveling in the opposite direction would gain speed. But this finding was contradictory to the results from Maxwell's equation, which suggested that light's speed is constant relative to the ether. It did not account for the observer's motion. This created an ambiguity about how an observer's motion through the ether affects measurements.

To test the ether hypothesis, Albert A. Michelson and Edward W. Morley conducted an experiment in 1887 at the Case School of Applied Science. The experiment used an interferometer, which split a light beam into two perpendicular paths, reflected them back with mirrors, and recombined them to produce an interference pattern (fringes). The interferometer could detect time differences as small as ~10^{-16} seconds, corresponding to a fringe shift of ~0.4 fringes if the ether wind existed at the Earth's orbital speed. It was rotated to align its arms at various angles relative to the Earth's motion. Observations were made at different times of day and over several months to account for changes in the Earth's velocity through the ether. It was expected that if the Earth moved through the ether, light along the arm parallel to the motion would take longer to travel (due to the ether wind) than light along the perpendicular arm. However, the experiment detected no significant fringe shift, with measured shifts less than 0.01 fringes, far below the expected ~0.4 fringes. This implied that the speed of light was constant in all directions, regardless of the Earth's motion through the ether. It suggested either that the ether was dragged along with the Earth (contradicting its stationary nature) or did not exist. Later in 1905, Albert Einstein's special relativity theory resolved the paradox by postulating that the speed of light is constant for all observers. Space and time were redefined as relative. The proof of the hypothesis in Newtonian physics signified the presence of philosophy in science.

In his 1933 lecture "On the Method of Theoretical Physics," Einstein stated, *"The axiomatic basis of theoretical physics cannot be extracted from experience but must be freely invented"*. Scientists propose a theory with certain assumptions, derive its implications, and then test those implications against experimental data. These assumptions involve ontological questions such as "what is the nature of reality?" as well as epistemological questions such as "how do we know what exists?".

An invention finds its inception in philosophy first, and then it takes form in physical reality. It was the philosophical understanding of emptiness or void that laid the groundwork for the mathematical adaptation of the number zero. Humans have always been fascinated with finding explicit expression for the implicit ideas in their minds. Like grammar of a language is an explicit discovery of the rules of the language. Mathematics is a tool based on a series of ideas and their relationship with each other.

Every generation builds upon the foundational work laid by the previous generation. And the field of machine learning is no different. But to envision a machine like a human, one first had to comprehend the nature of humans and how they interact with the environment they live in. Hence, the foundation principles behind the development of AI find their roots in the observation of laws and the development of a logical system of thinking to observe and interpret the findings. *The idea was never to create machines that are intelligent enough to pursue their objectives, but to build machines that will pursue our objectives.*

History

The science of Logic, or Nyāya, has been at the heart of Indian civilization from prehistoric times. It is said to have likely originated in the Vedic period (c. 1500–500 BCE) as a science of reasoning called Anvīkṣikī (the science of inquiry). The formal systematization of Nyāya is attributed to Akṣapāda Gautama (also known as Gotama or Gautama). While the exact date of composition of Nyāya Śāstra remains uncertain, scholarly estimates suggest the text was completed by the 2nd century CE, with evidence of later interpolations by scholars. Early commentators like Vātsyāyana (5th–6th century CE) wrote the Nyāya Bhāṣya, in which he clarified and expanded Gautama's sūtras. Uddyotakāra's Nyāyavārttika (6th–7th century CE) defended Nyāya against Buddhist critiques, while Vācaspati Miśra's Tātparyatīkā (9th century CE) and Udayana's Tātparyapariśuddhi and Nyāyakusumāñjali (10th century CE) refined logical and theistic arguments (Vidyabhusana 1990).

The science of Nyāya emphasized on rigorous approach to epistemology, through four valid means of knowledge (pramāṇa): perception (pratyakṣa), inference (anumāna), comparison (upamāna), and testimony (śabda). It emphasizes logical reasoning (tarka) and systematic debate (vāda-vidyā), and completely rejects uncritical reliance on intuition or scriptural authority. Perception is knowledge gained through direct sensory experience, such as seeing a tree. Inference is the knowledge preceded by perception and can be derived through reasoning based on observed correlations. For example, if one sees smoke, it can be inferred that there must be a fire from which the smoke originated. This relies on *vyāpti* (invariable concomitance), ensuring a universal relationship between the reason (*hetu*) and the inferred property (Chakrabarti 1999). Often it is described as a priori or a posteriori, or as a common scenario. A priori is the knowledge of the effect derived from the perception of its cause. For example, upon seeing the clouds, one can infer there will be rain. A posteriori is the knowledge of cause derived from the perception of its effect. For example, upon seeing a river swollen, one can conclude there was rain. Comparison is the knowledge of an entity based on its similarity to an entity already known. For example, a man travelling to the forest is told that in the forest roams a bison, which is quite similar to a cow. Upon confronting this creature in the forest, the man reaches the conviction that the animal he is seeing currently is a bison, based on the prior information about bison's similarity to a cow. Testimony is the instructive assertion of a reliable person or source. For example, before planning to visit a particular city, you make a phone call to a friend living in the city, who assures you of the favourable weather. Based on this testimony, you pack your belongings to suit the current weather.

The very idea of science implies the implicit use of logic, and from this point of view, all cultures that developed science must have had a system of logic. Back in the day, Greece was the philosophical center of the Western world. Although India and Greece had a long period of interaction that predates Alexander, there is no plausible evidence of Nyāya's influence on Greek philosophy or vice versa.

In the West, Greek philosophy began in Ionia, particularly in Miletus, during the 6th century BCE with the pre-Socratic philosophers, who sought to explain the universe through reason rather than mythology. Thales of Miletus (c. 624–546 BCE) proposed that water was the fundamental substance (*archē*) of all things. His thought process was rooted in observation that marked a departure from Homeric and Hesiodic myths, attributing natural phenomena to divine intervention (Curd 2019). Anaximander (c. 610–546 BCE), Thales' student, introduced the concept of the *apeiron* (the boundless) as the origin of all things, which offered a more abstract principle and created one of the earliest cosmological models. By the 5th century BCE, the Sophists emerged in Athens, a democratic hub where public speaking and persuasion were vital. Figures like Protagoras (c. 490–420 BCE) and Gorgias (c. 485–380 BCE) shifted philosophical focus from cosmology to human affairs, more about rhetoric, ethics, and epistemology. Protagoras' famous dictum, *"Man is the measure of all things,"* suggested a relativistic view of truth, where knowledge depends on individual perception (Kerferd 1981). Socrates (c. 470–399 BCE), though he left no writings, profoundly shaped Greek philosophy through his dialectical method. And his student Plato (427–347 BCE), who explored the nature of knowledge, reality, and reasoning, developed the dialectical method into a philosophical tool for ascending to knowledge of the Forms, which are eternal, immutable essences like Beauty or Justice. But it was his pupil, Aristotle (384–322 BCE), who was the first to formulate a precise set of laws governing the rational part of the mind and developed an informal system called *syllogistic logic*, now documented in the collection of six treatises, known as the *Organon* (Greek for tool or instrument). Aristotle established logic as a systematic discipline by exploring concepts like predication, contradiction, and the structure of propositions. A syllogism consists of two premises and a conclusion, such as "All men are mortal; Socrates is a man; therefore, Socrates is mortal".

He analysed how predicates (attributes or properties) are ascribed to subjects by distinguishing between essential predication (what a thing is in its essence, e.g., "A human is an animal") and accidental predication (non-essential attributes, e.g., "A human is tall"). In the Law of Non-Contradiction in Metaphysics (Book IV), Aristotle articulates that a proposition and its negation cannot both be true simultaneously (e.g., "It is raining" and "It is not raining" cannot both hold) (Aristotle 1924).

After Aristotle's death in 322 BCE, his school, the *Lyceum*, continued under Theophrastus (371–287 BCE), who expanded Aristotle's logical inquiries. In the Hellenistic period, Athens was a city alive with ideas. It was a hub of philosophical exchanges, where different schools of thought prospered and exchanged ideas. Apart from the *Lyceum*, Plato's *Academy* attracted philosophers from distant lands across the oceans. Zeno (334–262 BCE), a merchant-turned-philosopher from Citium in Cyprus, studied at the Academy under Polemo, its fourth head. While the Academy under Polemo focused less on formal logic than Plato's earlier metaphysical inquiries, it remained a place of rigorous debate, where students engaged with ideas from rival schools, including Aristotle's *Lyceum* (Diogenes Laertius 1925). Zeno most likely picked up on the idea of syllogism through these debates, but his education didn't stop at the Academy. He extended this pursuit of knowledge and logic with philosophers of the Megarian school, particularly Stilpo, whose logical skill and dialectical prowess by greatly admired by Zeno. The Megarians, heirs to Socrates' dialectical method, specialized in logical puzzles and paradoxes, such as the "liar paradox" and debates about implication. Although they were critical of some of the Aristotelian ideas, they engaged with the concepts and formed their own logical enquiries. Zeno absorbed the ideas from different domains and formed his own set of ideas, later known as *Stoicism*, which he began teaching at the Stoa Poikile, a painted colonnade in Athens' agora.

Zeno's Stoic logic, fully developed by Chrysippus (279–206 BCE), extended Aristotle's work by creating a propositional system that complemented Stoic cosmology and ethics. (Sedley 1999). The Stoics viewed logic as a core component of philosophy, alongside physics and ethics, calling it the "fence" that protects rational thought. They aimed to create a system that could rigorously analyse arguments in everyday reasoning, especially in ethical and cosmological contexts. Unlike Aristotle, who focused on scientific demonstration, the Stoics were *interested in practical reasoning, including conditionals like "If virtue is knowledge, then it can be taught."* This required a logic that could handle propositions as wholes, not just terms (Bobzien 2003). The Megarians' work on paradoxes (such as the "Liar Paradox") and modal concepts (such as possibility and necessity) prompted the Stoics to formalize propositional relationships to resolve such puzzles (William Kneale 1962).

However, the contributions to the system of logic came to an abrupt halt for a couple of centuries, due to the fall of the Roman Empire, but ideas floated around and across the land, and the literary works (especially of Aristotle) were preserved, translated, and rigorously analysed in other languages. Islamic philosopher Al-Farabi (870–950

CE) wrote extensive commentaries on the *Organon* and developed a logic system that integrated Aristotelian and Stoic elements and emphasized the structure of scientific demonstration. These translations and commentaries were picked by Avicenna, who wrote *Al-Shifa* (The Book of Healing), which included a comprehensive logical treatise reinterpreting Aristotle's Organon but refining the theory of the syllogism. Avicenna introduced modal logic (distinguishing necessary, possible, and impossible propositions) and developed a theory of hypothetical syllogisms (Tony Street 2016).

By the mid-12th century, James of Venice translated the complete works of Aristotle from Greek to Latin, making the full Organon available in the Latin West for the first time. Thomas Aquinas, a towering figure of scholasticism, further integrated Aristotelian logic into Christian theology. His commentaries on Aristotle's *"On Interpretation"* and *"Posterior Analytics"* clarified the principles of propositional structure and scientific demonstration. In his Summa Theologica, Aquinas employed syllogistic reasoning to construct theological arguments, demonstrating the harmony of faith and reason. His work exemplified the scholastic method of disputation, where logical rigor was used to resolve theological and philosophical questions. (Thomas Aquinas 2007).

Llull, born in Majorca (c. 1232), lived in a culturally diverse region and was educated in a scholastic context, and had access to Aristotle's complete logical system through these translations. The Organon's emphasis on structured argumentation influenced his desire to create a universal "art" of reasoning. In the published work *Ars Magna (1305)*, Ramon Lull presented his system of reasoning and later implemented a device made from set of paper wheels that could be rotated in various permutations. The Ars Magna was a radical departure from traditional logic, by mechanizing deduction in a way that anticipated modern computational approaches (Bonner 2007). By rotating the wheels, users could generate thousands of propositions, which Llull believed could reveal truths across disciplines and religions. His system was both a logical method and a missionary tool, designed to appeal to rational minds. After Llull's death, his Ars Magna gained followers in Europe, particularly in Catalonia and Italy. And any list of radical minds in human history would not skip mentioning the notable painter of Florence, who considered himself more of an engineer than a painter.

In the 16th century, Leonardo Da Vinci proposed the idea of a mechanical calculator through his sketches. His calculator concept involved gears and levers to perform arithmetic operations. But Vinci often left projects uncompleted and moved on to other propositions, which lured his creative mind (Laurenza 2006). His sketches for a mechanical calculator, though unrealized, fuelled the idea of automating arithmetic, and the first known working calculator was built around 1623 by Wilhelm Schickard (1592-1635) using gears to perform addition and subtraction. (Williams 1985). Now that the arithmetic process was automated, the very idea of automating the reasoning itself was not far from reach.

It was Thomas Hobbes (1588-1679) who first suggested, in Leviathan (1651), the idea of an 'artificial animal' which would do reasoning. In his understanding, reasoning was "nothing but reckoning", akin to adding and subtracting. (Stuart Russell n.d.).

Although the idea of formal logic is attested to the philosophers of ancient India, Greece, and China, the transformation to a formal science required the mathematization of logic and probability. The mathematical formulation of logic was inspired by the works of George Boole (1815-1864), which we now know as Boolean logic. Gottlob Frege later extended upon Boole's work to include objects and relations, which came to be known as the first-order logic and inspired the likes of Alan Turing.

The credit for igniting the mathematical development of probability, the theory of generalizing logic to circumstances with incomplete information, can be attributed to Gerolamo Cardano (1501-1576) and Blaise Pascal (1623-1662), who, in their respective time tried to frame the idea of probability in terms of possible events. But it was Thomas Bayes' idea of updating probabilities in the light of new evidence that became a cornerstone for Machine Learning later.

Ada Lovelace's collaboration with Charles Babbage on the Analytical Engine in the 19th century laid the foundation for modern programming. In 1843, Lovelace wrote an algorithm for the Analytical Engine, which is considered the first computer program. She recognized the potential of numbers and their ability to represent more than just numerical values, envisioning that machines could be programmed to perform complex calculations and manipulate symbols. Lovelace's algorithm for computing Bernoulli numbers showcased the concept of step-by-step instructions that could be executed by a machine, serving as a blueprint for modern programming. Her visionary ideas about the capabilities of computing machines and the significance of programming were ahead of their time. Although the Analytical Engine was never built during Lovelace's lifetime, her work and insights paved the way for future advancements in programming.

Ever since we (humans) developed mechanisms to store data, we have always tried to extract information from the data. Probability in combination with available data gave birth to a new field called *statistics*, the science of collecting, analysing, interpreting, and making inferences from data. Carl Friedrich Gauss (1777-1855) and Pierre-Simon Laplace (1749-1827) developed methods like the normal distribution and least squares, which later on became the foundation for data modelling.

But to truly replicate a model similar to the Human Brain, which could do analytical thinking and reasoning, it required a specialized study. But its mysteries have even eluded the great master of logic, Aristotle, who failed to deduce that the brain has anything to do with analytics and reasoning. It is a great irony indeed that the man who formalized the logical system simply discarded the importance of brain as an organ of minor importance and it was a direct attack on the correct view presented by Hippocrates (460–370 BCE), almost a century ago, who remarked in his work *On the Sacred Disease*, "*Men ought to know that from the brain, and from the brain only, arise our pleasures, joys, laughter, and jests, as well as our sorrows, pains, griefs, and tears. Through it, in particular, we think, see, hear, and distinguish the ugly from the beautiful, the bad from the good, the pleasant from the unpleasant... It is the same thing which makes us mad or delirious, inspires us with dread and fear, whether by night or by day, brings sleeplessness, inopportune mistakes, aimless anxieties, absent-mindedness, and acts that are contrary to habit".*

Nevertheless, Paul Broca (1824–1880) initiated the study of the brain's functional organization while investigating a case of speech deficiency. The fundamental nerve cells, *neurons*, were first observed individually by Camillo Golgi (1843–1926) through a staining technique. However, the measurement of brain activity began in 1929 with the invention of the electroencephalograph (EEG) device by Hans Berger (1873-1941).

The parallel works in different fields of science and mathematics collided eventually in 1943 when Warren McCulloch (1898-1969) and Walter Pitts (1923-1969) proposed a mathematical model of an artificial *neuron*, which could act as an on-off switch in response to the stimulus from neighbouring neurons. The McCulloch-Pitts neuron introduced the concept of binary threshold units that received inputs and produced outputs based on predefined activation thresholds. The neuron's output would only activate if the summed inputs crossed a specific threshold value. Later in 1949, Donald Hebb (1904-1985) demonstrated that the connection strength between artificial neurons can be updated, a rule which later came to be known as Hebbian learning.

Historically, adversity has fuelled invention, and World War II was such an adverse event that turned out to be a cornerstone for the development of A.I. During World War II, Alan Turing worked at Bletchley Park, developing the *Bombe*, a machine to decrypt German Enigma codes. His code-breaking algorithms used statistical and probabilistic techniques to infer patterns. In 1950, Alan Turing proposed the Turing Test, a criterion for machine intelligence. He suggested that a machine could be considered intelligent if it could convincingly imitate human behavior in a text-based conversation.

It was in 1957, when a psychologist and computer scientist at Cornell University, Frank Rosenblatt, proposed a computational model inspired by the 1943 McCulloch-Pitts neuron model, called Perceptron, which described artificial neurons as binary logic units. He implemented the perceptron model on an IBM 704 computer and demonstrated it as a pattern recognition system. It was one of the first models capable of supervised learning. (Rosenblatt n.d.)

Perceptron

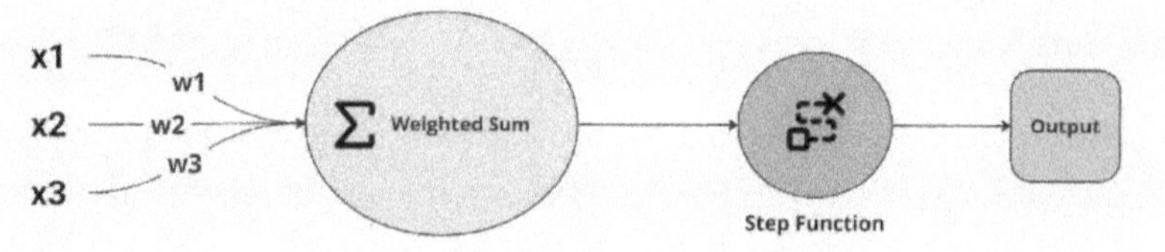

Figure 1 Perceptron Model

A perceptron (figure 1) receives multiple binary inputs, denoted as x_1, x_2, x_3, ..., where the value of each input can be either 0 or 1, and produces a single binary output. Additionally, there are corresponding weights w_1, w_2, w_3, ... associated with each input. The weights represent the importance or significance of each input in influencing the perceptron's output. The perceptron computes a weighted sum of the inputs and weights by multiplying each input by its corresponding weight and summing up these weighted values.

The perceptron then compares the weighted sum to a threshold value. The threshold is a parameter of the perceptron that determines the point at which the perceptron will "fire" and produce an output of 1. If the weighted sum is greater than or equal to the threshold, the perceptron outputs 1; otherwise, its output is 0. Following is its mathematical representation:

$$f(x) = \begin{cases} 1, & if \ w \cdot x + b > 0, \\ 0, & otherwise \end{cases}$$

$$w \cdot x = \sum_{i=1}^{m} w_i x_i$$

Here, w denotes a vector of real-valued weights, m is the number of inputs to the perceptron, and b is the bias. In addition to the weights and inputs, the perceptron model includes a bias term. The bias serves as an offset or a threshold that adjusts the decision boundary of the perceptron. It allows the perceptron to learn and generalize patterns that may not pass through the origin (0,0) in the input space. When combined with the weighted sum of inputs, the bias influences the point at which the perceptron transitions from producing output 0 to output 1. A positive bias makes it easier for the perceptron to output 1, while a negative bias makes it harder.

Consider that the perceptron defines a linear decision boundary, where points on one side of the hyperplane are classified as 1, and on the other as 0. The weights attached to the input determine the orientation of this hyperplane, while the bias shifts its position.

However, the model had its limitations and was heavily criticised by Marvin Minsky and Seymour Papert in their book, *Perceptrons: An Introduction to Computational Geometry (1969),* for its lack of ability to solve XOR problems and inability to model complex patterns. (Minsky n.d.) The basic perceptron model can only classify data that is linearly separable. It fails on the XOR problem, where outputs are 1 for inputs (0,1) or (1,0) and 0 for (0,0) or (1,1), which is not linearly separable. Minsky and Papert noted that even for linearly separable problems, the perceptron's learning algorithm could be slow or fail to converge if the data was noisy or poorly scaled. Since the perceptron was a single-layered model, they also suggested adding additional layers to model complex tasks would require infeasible computational resources given 1960s hardware. The criticism was to such a level that the perceptron model was even stopped from being considered in the research work related to the field of machine learning for nearly a decade.

The *perceptron* model breathed fresh air in 1986 when David Rumelhart, Geoffrey Hinton, and Ronald Williams addressed the perceptron's limitations in their paper *Learning Representations by Back-propagating Errors,* by enabling the training of multi-layer perceptrons (MLPs) through backpropagation (a concept introduced by Paul Werbos in 1974). The key idea behind backpropagation is to iteratively update the weights of the neural network using gradient descent. By calculating the gradients of the error with respect to the weights, the algorithm determines how much each weight contributes to the overall error and adjusts it accordingly.

$$w \leftarrow w - n \cdot \frac{\partial E}{\partial w}$$

Here, n is the learning rate, a hyperparameter that controls the step size of the weight update, and $\frac{\partial E}{\partial w}$ is the partial derivative of the loss function, E, with respect to the weight. A loss function quantifies the difference between the network's output and the true target. This iterative process continues until the network converges to a point where the error is minimized, and the network can make accurate predictions on unseen data. It generalizes the perceptron's learning rule to handle hidden layers, adjusting weights and biases to minimize prediction error.

The perceptron's step function was replaced with differentiable functions, known as *activation functions,* like sigmoid, tanh, and later ReLU, which allowed gradients to flow through the network and model non-linear patterns. This promoted the evolution of multi-layered networks and their application to real-world tasks,

There Is No A.I.

which was also complemented by an increase in the computational power of computers.

Neural Network

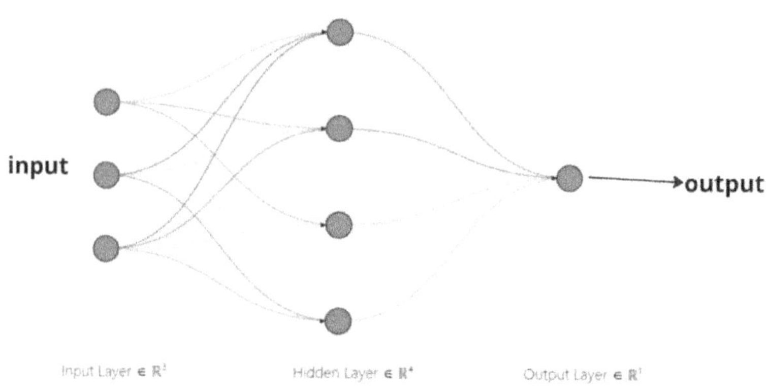

Figure 2 A multi-layer perceptron-based Neural Network

Figure 2 above represents a multi-layered perceptron model, where the first column of perceptrons, the *first layer,* weighs the input provided and passes the result to the second layer, the *hidden layer.* The hidden layer performs a similar act by weighing the evidence provided by the first layer and transmits its result to the final layer for final decision making as an output. The picture above is just for representational purposes, and for the sake of brevity, it has been kept simple and minimal. Since one layer transmits output to the other layer but does not receive any feedback, these models are also called *feed-forward neural networks (FFNN).* The number of perceptrons in a layer and the number of hidden layers from the first layer to and final layer can vary as per the complexity and requirement of the job at hand.

Prediction is always based on input. We do this activity commonly in daily life. For example, if there is a lot of humidity, we predict rain around the corner. Based on new government regulations, such as a tobacco ban, for instance, we predict the rise and fall of stock prices of a listed company selling tobacco-based products. In India, ITC is one such company whose stock price is always the talk of the town after the financial budget.

For a neural network to predict, it must process the data points passed to it as a set of observations or *input*. However, it is challenging to process information and generate predictions without prior knowledge. So, a neural network assigns weight to the information received. *The more data points we expose to our network, the more it optimizes its weight for reaching the desired output. It is an ever-continuous process where weights keep evolving.*

In essence, a neural network is a tool that looks for correlations between input and output datasets. However, in the real world, there will hardly be situations where input data will directly correlate with the output dataset. And just a one-layered neural network won't be enough to understand such relations. A neural network makes predictions based on the weights given to the input data points. If a certain input plays a dominant role in the outcome, it is given larger weight, and conversely, smaller weight is assigned if the input's role is less dominant. To find a correlation between input and output for correct prediction, we make a gradual adjustment in the network. Rather than just trying to figure out a direct correlation from input to output, we try to look for an intermediate state that has limited correlation with the output, and based on it, we try to predict the output. We call these intermediate states (s) layers *(s)*. Hence, multiple hidden layers are added to neural networks between the input layer and output layer to find relationships in complex scenarios. These hidden layers are nothing but different combinations of weights per scenario.

The rediscovery of the backpropagation algorithm allowed for the training of *multi-layer perceptrons (MLPs)*. This promoted deeper architectures, which enabled neural networks to learn complex features from data through successive layers of transformations. In the 1980s, the concept of convolutional layers in neural networks, inspired by the visual processing in the human brain's visual cortex, revolutionized image analysis by automatically learning hierarchical features from images, leading to breakthroughs in image recognition tasks.

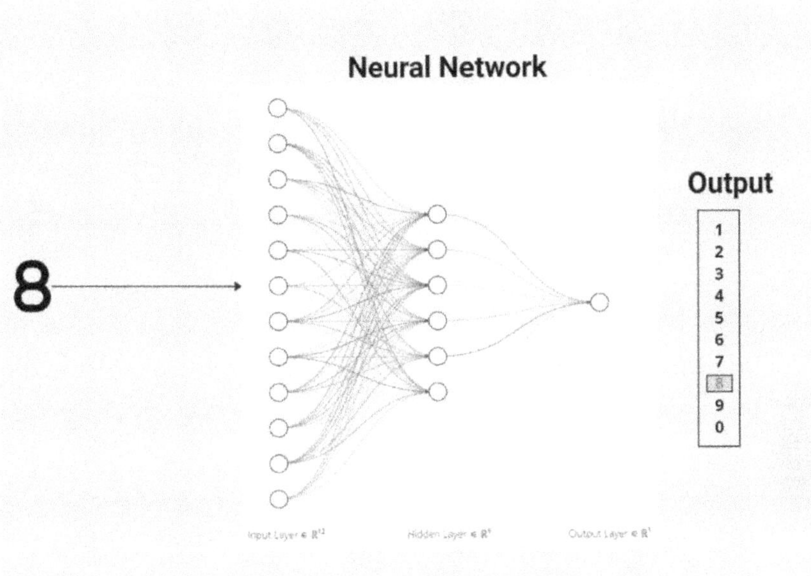

Figure 3 Neural Network - Image Classification

How to Train Your Network

To understand the context on a deeper level, it is necessary that we undertake this boring yet important journey to understand how a neural network is trained. This would give you a glimpse of all the magic in the background, and you will be able to relate to the discussion, which will be presented in further chapters of the book. And if you pass through this section, do give yourself a round of applause!

Step 1: Initialize random weights and biases:

At the beginning of training, the weights and biases of the neural network's individual neurons are set to random values. These weights determine the strength of connections between neurons and play a crucial role in the network's ability to learn and make predictions.

Step 2: Calculate an initial prediction by feed-forward:

Input data is fed into the network through the input layer. The data passes through the hidden layers, where weighted sums are computed and transformed by *activation functions*. These transformations generate an output prediction, which is compared to the desired target output. In a neural network, a single neuron's output calculation is a linear equation; however, in real life, data is non-linear. Activation functions inject the necessary nonlinearity into the network's computations, addressing a significant limitation in the original linear equations used for individual neurons.

Activation functions are mathematical functions applied to the output of each neuron. They introduce nonlinearity by introducing a curve or threshold that determines whether the neuron "fires" or becomes activated. This nonlinearity allows neural networks to approximate a wide range of functions, enabling them to model complex and nonlinear relationships within data.

The *sigmoid activation function* is often used to squash the output of a neuron into a bounded range, specifically between 0 and 1. This property makes it well-suited for tasks where the network's output needs to represent probabilities or binary classifications. By confining the output values within a limited range, the sigmoid function ensures that predictions remain within a meaningful and interpretable range.

While the sigmoid activation function does introduce some level of nonlinearity, it is less effective at combating the vanishing gradient. The *vanishing gradient problem* occurs when gradients become very small during backpropagation, leading to negligible updates to the network's parameters. This issue is particularly problematic for deep networks with many layers, as the gradients can diminish exponentially as they are propagated backward. When gradients are small, the network updates its parameters at a sluggish pace, effectively impeding the model's ability to learn from the data. This can result in networks that fail to capture complex patterns and fail to generalize well to new data.

Due to the vanishing gradient problem, using the sigmoid activation function between hidden layers is generally not recommended, especially for deep networks. Networks with multiple layers are more susceptible to vanishing gradients, which can lead to poor convergence and learning. As a result, more modern activation functions, such as ReLU and its variants (Leaky ReLU, Parametric ReLU), have become more popular choices for hidden layers. These functions address the vanishing gradient issue more effectively and enable faster convergence.

ReLU, or Rectified Linear Unit, is a widely used activation function in neural networks. Its fundamental purpose is to introduce nonlinearity into the network's computations. Despite its simplicity, *ReLU's* effectiveness in adding nonlinearity makes it a crucial component for enabling neural networks to model and capture complex patterns and relationships within data. *ReLU* helps mitigate the vanishing gradients problem by allowing positive gradients to flow through unaffected.

While *ReLU* does prevent vanishing gradients, it can contribute to the exploding gradient problem in certain situations. When the network's weights are initialized with large values, *ReLU* can cause activations to explode, leading to large gradients during backpropagation.

Batch normalization is a technique that normalizes the activations within a layer by adjusting the mean and variance. This normalization can help prevent activations from becoming too large and contribute to more stable training.

When compared to other activation functions, such as sigmoid or tanh, *ReLU* requires fewer computational resources. This efficiency is valuable, especially in scenarios involving large datasets and deep networks, where computational demands can be significant.

Step 3: Calculate the network's error based on a differentiable metric:

Metrics help us analyse what's working, what's not, and what could be the reason behind it. In machine learning, metrics are used as tools to set standards and evaluate the performance of models. Having a functional model is nowhere near the job done flag post. Neural network models do not solve the problem directly but try to approximate it by optimizing a specific task. To do that, the model must be adjusted, appropriately guided, and monitored. And this is where metrics help us to determine how well models are performing on tasks that are given to them.

A loss function or error metric is chosen to quantify the difference between the predicted output and the actual target. Loss functions are used as tools to optimize a model's parameters during its training phase. It measures the difference between the predicted and expected outputs of the model, and the overall goal is to minimize this difference. This differentiability is a vital property that allows us to calculate the derivative of the loss function concerning the network's parameters. The gradient of the loss function concerning the parameters indicates how the loss changes as the parameters are adjusted. This provides a way to measure how well a model is learning during the training process by calculating the deviation of predictions from correct values. Loss functions map a scenario (consisting of one or many values) onto a real number that represents the loss, cost, risk, or error of that scenario. In practical terms, if a set of predictions is far from the set of true labels, the loss function should output a higher value, and conversely, accurate predictions should result in lower loss values. A model is considered sufficiently trained when the loss has been minimized below a predetermined threshold.

The gradients obtained from these derivatives are utilized in gradient descent, an optimization technique that systematically adjusts the parameters to minimize the loss function. This process facilitates efficient and organized exploration of the loss landscape, enabling the network to gradually converge to a set of parameter values that result in improved predictions.

A loss function takes two inputs: the model's prediction and the actual ground-truth value. It computes a measure of the discrepancy between the prediction and the true value, quantifying how well the model's output aligns with reality. This measure serves as an indicator of the quality of the model's predictions, guiding the optimization process.

Common loss functions include mean squared error (MSE) for regression tasks and cross-entropy for classification tasks. The goal is to minimize this error during training.

Although loss functions and metrics both evaluate model performance, they serve different purposes in the AI/ML pipeline at different stages. While loss functions are used during the training phase for parameter optimization, metrics are used once the model is trained and are subjected to unseen data. The primary use of metrics is for the evaluation and comparison of different models on a desired task. It would be fair to say that metrics evaluate a model's generalization capabilities after the training phase.

Selecting an appropriate Loss function is one of the most crucial decisions while designing an AI/ML system. Let us consider a scenario where we are calculating the average salary of people sitting in a room. The output will be a reasonable number; however, if a very rich person enters the room, the average salary skyrockets, even though the typical person's salary hasn't changed. So, we learn that using the MSE (Mean Squared Error) alone can be misleading when extreme outliers exist. Functions like Huber Loss or Quantile Loss might be better suited in such cases with outliers.

The loss function defines how a model learns from its mistakes by quantifying the difference between predictions and actual values. If the function poorly represents the error, it can lead to slow learning of the model. Since models update their weights based on the gradient of the loss function, if the gradients grow exponentially during backpropagation, the model's weight/parameter updates may overshoot the optimal values and will result in wild oscillations in training. To fix it, we may consider limiting the gradient magnitude to a fixed range or using smaller learning rates with proper weight initialization techniques.

Conversely, if the gradients shrink exponentially, making weight updates too small, models suffer from repeated multiplication of small gradients. This severely limits the learning rate of a model. For instance, suppose we use sigmoid activation in multiple layers. Since its derivative is at most 0.25, multiplying many small derivatives results in almost zero gradients in earlier layers, which means they learn slowly. Alternatively, we can use the *ReLU* activation function, as it does not saturate like sigmoid or tanh, thus reducing the risk of vanishing gradients.

Notably, loss functions are sensitive to different types of errors, and based on the sensitivity, it may influence the model to overfit or underfit. If the sensitivity of a loss function is high, it will penalize even small errors harshly, which means the model is focusing on minute details and, in turn, is over-optimized. The model may not be able to learn meaningful patterns in the longer run and may fit noise instead. It is kind of a rule of thumb that *Mean*

Squared Error (MSE) is commonly used in regression tasks, but is not ideal for classification problems.

There are many possibilities when it comes to choosing the right metric for evaluating a business-specific goal, as there is always an opportunity to tailor a custom metric for a specific business domain, which broadens the scope in comparison to loss functions. A well-chosen metric will ensure that the model optimizes for business goals rather than misleading or irrelevant indicators. However, it has to be noted that even with the right metric, business success isn't guaranteed due to external factors like data quality, deployment issues, and evolving requirements.

Let us take a problem statement where a bank wants to develop a fraud detection system to detect fraudulent credit card transactions. The underlying business goal would be to "minimize fraud while ensuring that legitimate transactions are not wrongly flagged".

Fraud detection systems deal with class imbalance, where fraudulent transactions are significantly fewer than legitimate ones. In this case, to test a model's performance, it would be unwise to use accuracy as a metric. If the model predicts all transactions as non-fraud, it will still achieve 99% accuracy, but completely fail at detecting fraud.

Precision and recall are two metrics that are commonly used in fraud detection cases; however, if we analyse deeply, they are not always ideal. Precision measures how many transactions labelled as fraud are fraudulent.

$$Precison = \frac{TP}{TP + FP}$$

Precision considers both fraud and non-fraud cases, but fraud detection is not just about fraud; it is also about minimizing false positives (FPR). It alone does not tell us if we are missing fraud cases (false negatives). A highly precise model might be overly conservative and only flag fraud when it is 100% sure, missing many actual fraud cases (high false negatives).

Suppose we tweak the fraud detection model to be highly precise (Precision = 0.99). There is a good possibility that it will detect only 50% of frauds to reduce false positives. Now consider the impact that fewer legit transactions are blocked, while many fraudsters may go undetected, which in turn leads to financial losses.

Recall measures how many fraudulent transactions were correctly detected.

$$Recall = \frac{TP}{TP + FN}$$

A high recall means catching most frauds, but it often comes at the cost of more false positives. A model that detects 95% of fraud (TPR = 0.95) but also falsely flags 5% of legit transactions as fraud (FPR = 0.05) can create millions of false alarms daily in high-volume systems.

A large-scale payment system may handle millions or billions of transactions per day, and fraudulent transactions can be just 0.001% of the transactions recorded in a day. Instead of only optimizing for precision and recall, an alternate strategy in high-scale fraud detection would be to set high specificity and maximize recall. Specificity (True Negative Rate, TNR) is a metric that measures how well a model correctly identifies non-fraudulent (legitimate) transactions.

$$Specificity = \frac{TN}{TN + FP}$$

To reduce false positives in large-scale fraud detection where billions of transactions are happening daily, we set Specificity = 0.999999 (meaning only 1 false positive per million transactions). This helps to prevent over-flagging legitimate transactions and ensures only a tiny fraction of legitimate transactions get mistakenly flagged. The goal is to detect as many fraud cases as possible (high recall) without falsely flagging too many legitimate transactions (high specificity). If we maximize recall within high specificity, maximum fraud cases will be detected without overwhelming false positives.

Moreover, with adaptive thresholding for different scenarios, such as a new user doing a large transaction or a transaction happening from an unusual device, etc. We can even go for a cascading model approach, where the primary model (High Specificity, Low Recall) is a conservative model that flags only the most obvious fraud cases, and the second model analyses transactions that the first model didn't flag. No doubt this is a costlier approach (computationally as well as latency-wise), but the trade-off is higher accuracy with fewer false positives (FP), which reduces operational costs in the long run.

Step 4: Adjust the values of weights and biases using backpropagation:

Backpropagation is a process that calculates the gradients (derivatives) of the loss function concerning the network's parameters. These gradients are computed by propagating the error backward through the network, layer by layer. A gradient indicates the direction and magnitude of adjustments needed to minimize the error. The obtained gradients indicate the direction and magnitude of changes needed in the parameters to reduce the loss. During each iteration of the optimization process, the parameters are updated in the direction opposite to the gradient, gradually steering the model towards more accurate predictions.

The word *gradient* in English means *'a part sloping upward or downward'*. When we are trying to reduce or eliminate errors, we are trying to reach a stable ground truth, similar to a ball rolling down the hill or a man trying to climb up. In order to either reach the bottom or top, both the ball and man may take longer strides initially, but as they reach closer to the target, their steps will get smaller and smaller to avoid overshooting it. In this context, the gradient is a vector that contains the direction of the steepest step a ball or man can take and how long that step should be.

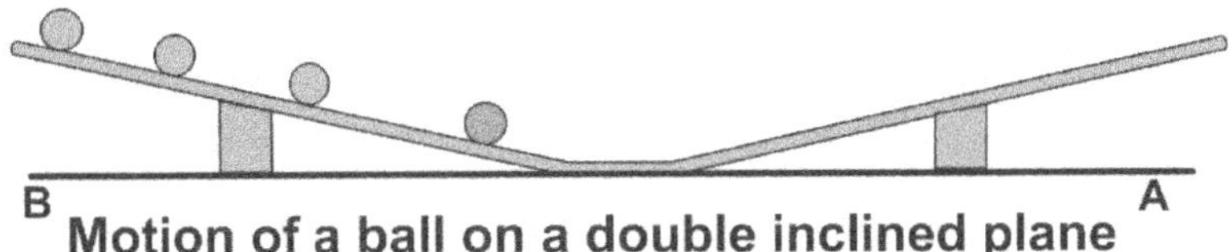

Motion of a ball on a double inclined plane

In order to observe the steepness of a slope, we start from any starting point and then find the derivative to measure the steepness and direction of the slope. This is what we do in linear regression problems to find the line of best fit. Gradient Descent aims to minimize the error (or loss function) between the predicted value and the actual output. And to do so, it requires a *direction* and a *learning rate* (the size of steps to be taken to reach the minimum point).

In the early phase of training a neural network, the weights are far from the optimal solution, and the gradient descent provides only a rough direction to reduce the loss. Hence, scaling helps the model cover more ground in the loss landscape quickly in order to find regions of lower error. *Learning rate* is the scaling factor that controls the magnitude of the weight updates to ensure that the network learns at a controlled and stable pace. However, as training progresses and the model gets closer to the optimal solution, the gradients become smaller since the loss function flattens near the minimum.

Mathematically, for a function $f(x_1, x_2 ..., x_n$ The gradient is denoted as:

$$\nabla f = (\frac{\partial f}{\partial x_1}, \frac{\partial f}{\partial x_2}, ... \frac{\partial f}{\partial x_n})$$

Each component of the gradient vector represents the partial derivative of the function with respect to the corresponding input variable. The gradient provides the direction of the fastest increase in the function's value from a specific point in the input space.

In the context of optimization, such as in gradient descent, the negative gradient (opposite direction of the gradient) is used to move towards the minimum of a function. By iteratively adjusting the parameters in the direction opposite to the gradient, the optimization algorithm aims to find the minimum (or maximum) value of the function.

Optimization algorithms, such as *stochastic gradient descent (SGD)* or its variants, use these gradients to update the weights and biases iteratively, nudging the network parameters toward values that reduce the error.

Step 5: Repeat until the desired accuracy is reached:

Steps 2 to 4 are repeated iteratively for a predetermined number of epochs or until a specific accuracy threshold is achieved. The network continues to refine its weights and biases, gradually improving its performance on the training data. It's essential to monitor the validation performance to avoid overfitting (excessive adaptation to the training data) and achieve a balance between training and generalization. A validation set, separate from the training set, is used to monitor the model's performance during training. This helps prevent overfitting. Training can be stopped early if the model's performance on the validation set starts to degrade, indicating that it's no longer learning useful patterns.

Recurrent Neural Network

Later, a specialized type of neural network came into existence, which took into consideration the concept of time and sequence, recurrent neural networks (RNNs). RNNs evolved to address a key limitation of FFNNs: their lack of temporal or sequential processing. RNNs were designed to model sequences and time-series, where the order of inputs matters, such as in language (where word order affects meaning) or stock prices (where past values influence future trends).

RNNs take their inspiration from the Hopfield network designed by Mr. John Hopfield in 1982, who was recently awarded the Physics Nobel Prize 2024 for constructing methods that helped lay the foundation for today's powerful machine learning. The Hopfield network draws its strength by mimicking the associative memory function of the brain by introducing recurrent connections, where each neuron feeds back to others, and hence the network can maintain the state and converge to stored patterns.

To put it in simple terms, imagine recalling an unusual word which we use rarely, such as one for the supportive structure for a rider of an animal. We scan the words stored in the memory. It is something like what was that word? syll..able?? Umm.. no.. it is 'saddle'. This is how the associative memory function of our brain looks. The Hopfield network can store patterns and has a method for recreating them. When the network is given an incomplete or slightly distorted pattern, the method can find the stored pattern that is most similar.

Say, we feed the network with two simple 3x3 images with the following patterns: Pattern 1: and Pattern 2:

$$\text{Pattern 1:} \begin{bmatrix} 1 & -1 & 1 \\ 1 & 1 & -1 \\ -1 & 1 & -1 \end{bmatrix} \text{ and Pattern 2:} \begin{bmatrix} -1 & 1 & -1 \\ 1 & -1 & 1 \\ 1 & 1 & -1 \end{bmatrix}$$

And then we present the network with an incomplete version of Pattern 1:

$$\text{Incomplete Pattern:} \begin{bmatrix} 1 & -1 & 1 \\ ? & 1 & -1 \\ -1 & ? & ? \end{bmatrix}$$

The network will use stored patterns to recreate/complete the image. Let us understand how this works.

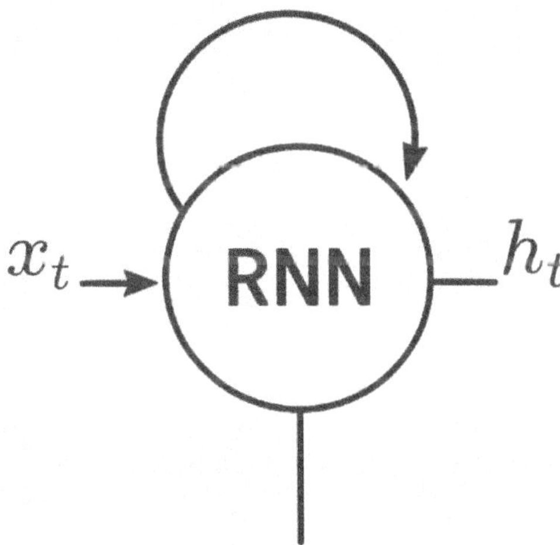

Figure 4 A Recurrent Neural Network (RNN) neuron

Here, x_t is the input vector at time step t. It enters the RNN neuron and influences the current output. h_t is the hidden state or output at time step t, computed by the RNN. It captures both the new input and the memory from the previous state. The looped arrow going from the output back into the RNN neuron represents the recurrence, the ability to use its previous state, h_{t-1} , as input for the next step. This recurrence ability enables the RNN to handle sequences and maintain memory over time.

Each neuron in the network is a binary unit, taking states of +1 (active) or -1 (inactive), similar to the perceptron's binary output but operating in a recurrent context. Each pair of neurons in a fully connected network is connected by a weight (represented by the weight between the ith and j^{th} neuron), which represents how their states are correlated across different patterns. These correlations are captured through a learning rule (like Hebbian learning, i.e., *neurons that fire together, wire together*) and stored in the weight matrix.

To put it simply, the weights are adjusted according to the correlation between the states of neurons in the patterns. So, if neurons i^{th} and j^{th} tend to be in the same state in many patterns, the weight between them will be positive, indicating that these neurons should support each other's states. However, if they tend to be in opposite states, the weight will be negative, an indication to adopt opposite states.

The weights across the network are symmetric, and there are no self-connections. The idea here is to use the values of these weights to determine how the neurons collectively behave, and by adjusting these weights, we can store patterns in the network. Each pattern (e.g., text, image, etc.) is encoded by adjusting the weights in such a way that the neurons in that pattern have strong correlations, making the pattern an *attractor state* of the network, a state that the network naturally falls into when given similar or incomplete information. The weights are adjusted so that the pattern represents a low-energy configuration.

The idea here is that when the network is given an input that is close to the stored pattern (even if some neurons are missing or incorrect), the network will naturally gravitate towards the full pattern during recall. The dynamics of the system will push it toward this low-energy state, effectively reconstructing the stored pattern.

In a nutshell, when we present a partial or noisy version of a stored pattern, the weights (which store the correlations between neurons) guide the neurons back to the correct configuration. Neurons that are supposed to be positive in the full pattern will get positive inputs from their connected neighbours, and those that are supposed to be negative will get negative inputs. The stored weights act like a memory of the patterns.

The system is designed in such a way that each pattern corresponds to a minimum in the network's energy landscape. A high-energy state corresponds to a random, noisy, or incomplete pattern where the neurons' activations are far from one of the stored patterns. On the contrary, a low-energy state corresponds to a stable state, or the attractor state discussed earlier.

When an incomplete pattern is presented, the dynamics of the network pull the neurons into one of these minima, restoring the original pattern. A similar analogy can be thought of in terms of a ball rolling down into a valley in a landscape. As the neurons update their states, the network slides down towards the nearest valley. Once it reaches the bottom, it stays there. Here, the bottom corresponds to a low-energy state (or one of the stored patterns).

Training RNNs requires propagating errors across time steps, a challenge Hopfield Networks avoided with unsupervised Hebbian learning. *Backpropagation Through Time (BPTT)*, developed in the 1980s and formalized by Werbos (1990), adapts the backpropagation strategy to RNNs and enables supervised learning of sequential data. (Werbos n.d.)

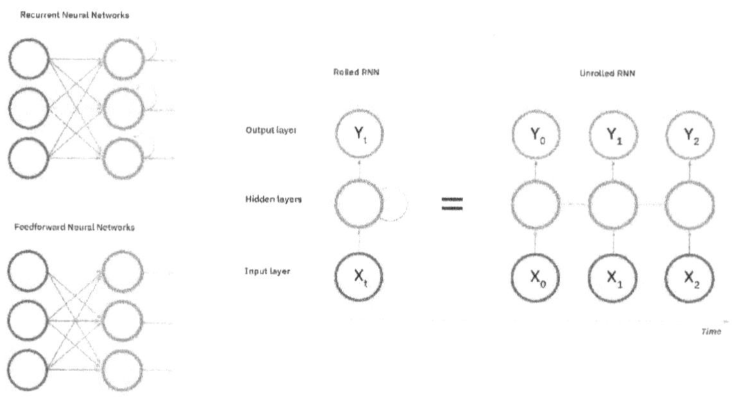

Figure 5 RNN vs FFNN (source:
https://www.ibm.com/think/topics/recurrent-neural-networks)

And it is the sequential processing ability of RNNs that proved crucial to propel the neural networks from just predicting about data to cross the barrier and generate the data, a significant milestone for days to come. RNNs, such as LSTM (Long Short-Term Memory) or GRU (Gated Recurrent Unit), are often used as the building blocks of the encoder-decoder model.

The encoder takes in the input sequence and processes it step by step, producing a fixed-size context vector or hidden state that captures the information from the entire input sequence. The last hidden state of the encoder serves as the initial hidden state for the decoder.

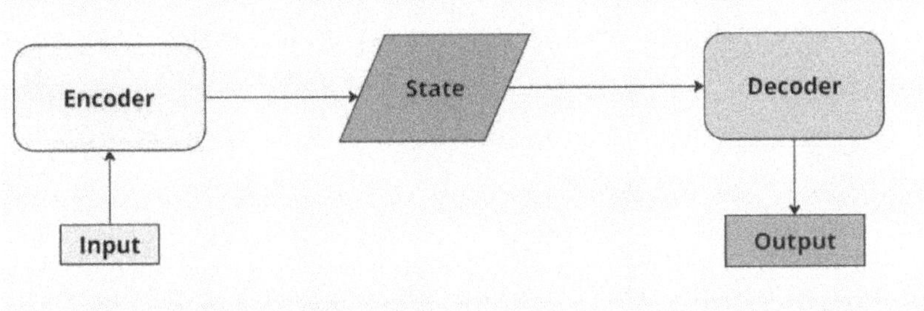

Figure 6 Encoder Decoder Model

The decoder generates the output sequence step by step based on the context vector and the previously generated tokens. Similar to the encoder, RNNs are used in the decoder. At each time step, the decoder generates a token and updates its hidden state using both the context vector and the previously generated token. This process continues until an end-of-sequence token is generated or a maximum sequence length is reached.

Say, an input sentence is encoded into a single context vector that is used as the initial hidden state for the decoder. These hidden states capture the context and information of the input sequence as a whole. However, as the input sentence becomes longer, compressing all the information into a single vector can lead to a loss of detailed information. Long sentences may have complex structures and distant associations that are challenging to capture effectively within this single context vector.

Natural language sentences can have complex structures and dependencies that span long distances. These dependencies are crucial for proper translation or generation. Encoding such complex structures into a single vector can lead to inefficiencies and a lack of expressive power to capture all the nuances of the source sentence. Long sequences pose challenges due to the vanishing gradient problem. RNNs struggle to capture long-range dependencies, which is important for tasks like machine translation.

During the decoding phase, while generating the output sequence, the decoder can leverage these hidden states from the encoder. Each time step in the decoder's generation process can be influenced by different hidden states from the encoder. This allows the decoder to access and incorporate the relevant context information from the input sequence as needed.

Even though the architecture of RNN is much closer to our brain functioning, they have not had much adaptation in comparison to FFNNs, and Feed-forward neural networks remain the popular choice of data scientists. During BPTT, gradients can shrink (vanishing gradient) or grow (exploding gradient) exponentially over long sequences, which makes it difficult to learn long-term dependencies. Moreover, the process itself is computationally expensive. Some specific RNN models, such as Long Short-Term Memory (LSTMs) (Hochreiter n.d.)and Gated Recurrent Units (GRUs) (Cho n.d.) use gating mechanisms to preserve long-term dependencies, but these add complexity and computational cost.

Although FFNNs are popular, the Hopfield Network and RNNs remain influential to this date. Its energy-based framework inspires diffusion models (e.g., DALL·E 3) and neuromorphic computing by leveraging recurrence for efficiency. Currently, RNNs are mostly used in niche applications like time-series (e.g., stock prediction), speech processing, and robotics, where sequential dynamics are critical.

Rise of Transformers

RNNs, although powerful for their time, were limited by the amount of compute and memory needed to perform well at generative tasks. With a significant increase in input data, RNNs require significant scaling of resources for the model. We must understand, for text predicting tasks in natural languages like English, a model needs to have an understanding of the language, as in many languages, one word can have multiple meanings. Hence, models need to understand the context of the input before generating reasonable text, and to achieve this require significant training data, and in the case of RNNs, this became quite a limitation. And to address such limitations, attention mechanisms were introduced.

An *attention mechanism* is a computational method inspired by the human visual attention system, which allows neural networks and models to focus on specific parts of input data while processing information. The core idea of an attention mechanism involves associating different weights or attention scores with various elements of the input. These scores determine the relative importance of different elements during the computation.

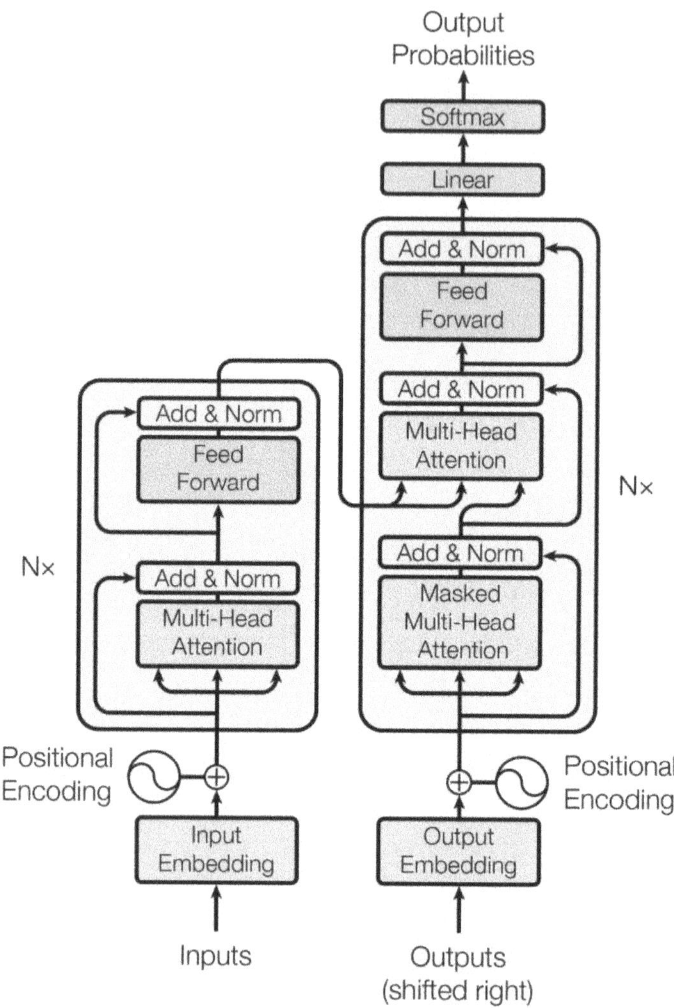

Figure 7 Transformer Architecture (Source:
https://arxiv.org/abs/1706.03762)

process. It helps the models to focus on relevant information and thus enhances their ability to capture important relationships and patterns. In tasks involving long sequences, attention mechanisms mitigate the vanishing gradient problem, which allows the model to capture dependencies across distant elements.

In 2017, a revolutionary paper *"Attention Is All You Need"* was published by Google researchers, which proposed the Transformer architecture, and it revolutionized the way neural networks process sequential data, by addressing some of the limitations of RNNs and LSTMs (Ashish Vaswani 2017). Transformers can be scaled efficiently to use multi-core GPUs, and they can parallelly process input data thus making use of much larger training datasets.

To understand the significance of *"Attention Mechanism"*, which is the core part of the A.I. models nowadays, usually known as *Large Language Models (LLMs)*, we take a use case.

Say, we want to develop a translation model that can translate text from one language to another. Language translation is not a straightforward process. One needs to understand the context and frame the words accordingly. A plain word-by-word translation may look a bit awkward. For example:

French: *Le battage médiatique quotidien autour des modèles d'IA me semble assez écrasant.*

Word by Word Translation:

Le battage — The Hype; Médiatique — media; Quotidien — daily; Autour — around; Des — some; Modèles — models; d'IA — AI; me — me; semble — seems; assez — enough; écrasant — crushing

Actual English Interpretation: *The daily media hype around AI models seems pretty overwhelming to me.*

Earlier, recurrent neural networks (RNNs) were the most preferrable choice for implementing language translation using an encoder-decoder architecture.

RNN-based encoder-decoder architecture models process text sequences one step (word) at a time, maintaining a temporally linked hidden state that gets updated at each step (word). The hidden state is used to capture information from previous steps (words). Thus, the final hidden state serves as a compressed representation of the entire text sequence, often represented as a context vector, which serves as the initial hidden state for the decoder. The decoder then generates an output sequence (prediction) autoregressively by conditioning each prediction on the previous hidden state. In simpler terms, each predicted word is fed back into the decoder to generate the next word.

And herein lies the shortcoming which we were talking about. The RNN model can't directly access earlier hidden states from the encoder during the decoding phase. It has to solely rely on the current hidden state, which encapsulates all relevant information. Since neural networks use gradient descent and gradients diminish during backpropagation through time, there is a strong possibility of a loss of context, especially in complex sentences, where the model must learn long-range dependencies. As a result, important words appearing earlier in the sequence may be forgotten by the time the decoder needs them. Moreover, since this process is sequential, which leads to $O(n)$ time complexity for sequence length n, the advantage of leveraging parallel computation is out of the box.

The real pain point was the single context vector or the final hidden state of the encoder phase, which acted as the sole entry point to the decoder phase. The transformers, through their attention mechanism, allow the decoder to access all encoder hidden states through a learned alignment model. At each step, attention weight relative to the encoder hidden state is computed, which indicates the relevance of the encoder state. This step is called the "Self-attention" mechanism.

Self-attention mechanism allows each position in the text sequence to consider the relevance of other positions. Let us consider the sentence:

"The cat chased the mouse because it was hungry."

While processing the above text sentence, the model should be able to understand that the word 'it' in the above sentence is referring to the cat and not the mouse. In a transformer-based architecture, it is the attention mechanism that makes that determination. It is quite unlike the earlier RNN-based architecture, which was unidirectional in flow. The attention mechanism helps the decoder to retroactively retrieve encoder states from any position. But how does the decoder learn to pay attention to relevant states?

The attention mechanism involves two main steps:

1. Relevance scoring: Scoring the relevancy of previous tokens concerning the current token being processed. Higher scores indicate stronger semantic or syntactic relationships between tokens. For example, in the sentence *"The cat chased the mouse because it was* *hungry*", processing "*chased*" yields high scores with "*cat*" (subject) and "*rat*" (object), which throws light on verb-argument dependencies.

One of the popular ways of computing the scores is by using the scaled dot-product attention mechanism. It computes contextual representations by dynamically weighting input tokens through three core components — queries (Q), keys (K), and values (V) — and a critical scaling operation.

A Query (Q) represents the token seeking contextual information, Key (K) represents all tokens in the sequence that the Query token can attend to, and Value (V) contains the actual content of the tokens, which will be weighted and combined based on attention scores.

Once the attention score is calculated using a dot-product similarity, the score needs to be scaled so that the variance of the dot-product values remains controlled and does not unnecessarily produce extremely large values. The scaled attention scores are passed through a Softmax function to convert them into probabilities. This function ensures that all attention scores sum to 1, making it easier for the model to distribute focus across multiple tokens.

Let us simplify the above sentence and see this process in action: Input Sentence: The cat chased the mouse.

$$Attention\ Score = Q_i . K_t^j$$

Let us assume the attention score between "chased" (i^{th} Query) and other words (Keys, ranging from j to T) is as follows: [0.58, 0.94, 1.85, 0.89, 1.45]. Now, we scale the score around the given dimensionality of the embedding space.

$$Scaled\ Attention\ Score = \frac{QK^T}{\sqrt{d_k}}$$

Here, d_k is the dimensionality of the embedding space.

If we approximate the above attention scores for a 3-dimensional embedding space, the revised values that we get are [0.33, 0.54, 1.07, 0.51, 0.84]. To convert these scores into probabilities, we use a Softmax function. These probabilities determine how much weight each Value vector (V) should have in the final output. This tells us the likelihood of each word being the next word in the sentence. Among all these probabilities, one word(token) will have the highest probability (greedy decoding).

Say, once we apply the Softmax function, the calculations w.r.t each word come as follows: [0.11, 0.14, 0.27,0.13, 0.21]. This means that the word "*chased*" accounts for 27% of itself, 21% to "*mouse*", and so on.

This process can be independently and in parallel repeated for all words in the sentence to form their new contextual representations.

2. Contextual Integration: The above calculated scores are then used to compute a weighted sum of the value (V) vectors, which helps to form the output representation for the token, incorporating relevant information from all input tokens.

$$Attention\ output = \sum (Attention\ Weight \times V)$$

The final resulting vector corresponding to the word *"chased"* will be a blend of information from the other words in the sentence, weighted by their importance. Instead of a static meaning, relationships are now being captured in the output vector.

No wonder, the attention calculation is the most computationally expensive part of the LLM process. And to make this part more efficient, numerous improvement algorithms are being incorporated to smooth out the process and make the output more relevant. The approach discussed so far computes only one set of attention weights, which means it captures just one type of relationship in a sentence. Hence, to add diversification to the model, multi-head attention mechanisms are used.

In a multi-head mechanism, several attention mechanisms are applied in parallel to capture different relationships, such as subject-verb, object-action, long-distance dependencies, etc. This makes the final output vector richer and more informative. The outputs of these heads are concatenated and linearly transformed to produce the final self-attention output. The count of attention heads in the attention layer varies from model to model, but numbers in the range of 12-100 are common. The idea here is that each self-attention head will learn a different aspect of language. Say, one set might learn the relationship of entities in the sentence, while another set focuses on the activity.

The original Transformer model had only 6 encoder and decoder layers. Each encoder and decoder layer contained a multi-head self-attention mechanism (8 attention heads per layer). Recent models have hundreds of layers and hundreds of attention heads stacked on top of each other. A year later, in 2018, Google introduced **BERT,** based on the transformer architecture, which brought a breakthrough in NLP by introducing bidirectional pretraining. Prior to BERT, most language models were trained to process text in one direction only, either left-to-right or right-to-left. This made it difficult for them to capture the full context of a sentence, as they could only see the words that came before or after the current word.

BERT considers both directions, capturing richer contextual information. This significantly improved the quality of contextual embeddings, benefiting tasks like language understanding, sentiment analysis, and more. For example, on the GLUE benchmark, which is a suite of natural language processing tasks, BERT achieved state-of-the-art results on 11 of the 12 tasks. This includes tasks such as question answering, natural language inference, and sentiment analysis.

BERT's bidirectional pretraining enables the model to learn the contextual relationships between words that appear in different parts of a sentence. This is essential for disambiguating words with multiple meanings and for understanding how words influence each other's interpretation within a given context. For example, the word "bank" can refer to a financial institution or the side of a river, and BERT can learn which meaning is more likely based on the surrounding words.

One of the limitations of traditional models that process text sequentially, such as RNNs, is their inability to capture long-range dependencies effectively. While RNNs can be used for generative AI tasks, they struggle with compute and memory, making it hard to keep context in longer texts. The transformer's architecture is more parallelizable, and its dynamic attention mechanism helps to capture long-range dependencies in the input. BERT overcomes this limitation by considering words that are not adjacent to each other in the sentence. For instance, BERT can learn that words like "love" and "hate" are often associated, even if they appear in separate sentences. This ability to capture relationships between distant words is crucial for understanding the overall sentiment, tone, and meaning of a piece of text.

Bidirectional pretraining allows BERT to learn more complex representations of words. For example, BERT can learn that the word "bank" can have multiple meanings, depending on its context. BERT's contextual embeddings contribute to its effectiveness across a wide range of NLP tasks, making it a foundational model for modern natural language processing and Generative AI.

Transformers, with their attention mechanisms and parallel processing capabilities, opened the door to improved performance on a wide array of NLP tasks that had previously posed challenges for traditional RNN-based models. The key breakthrough lay in their remarkable ability to capture contextual relationships among words in a sentence. Unlike older models that processed text sequentially, Transformers could simultaneously weigh the significance of each word in relation to every other word in the input sequence. This holistic contextual understanding paved the way for more nuanced comprehension and generation of language. In the context of Generative AI, the Transformers became a catalyst for the development of LLMs. Large Language models, based upon the Transformer architecture, put the generative capabilities in top gear.

Generative AI models, such as those based on the Transformer architecture, have made it possible for individuals and organizations to harness the power of AI-generated content and creativity without requiring an in-depth understanding of data science or machine learning. These models allow users to generate text, images, music, and more, expanding the scope of creative expression and content generation. The outputs generated by these AI models are often remarkable in their creativity, accuracy, and coherence.

End Note

We have covered a lot of ground so far by briefly navigating the landscape of A.I. evolution. We know the functioning details that power the current A.I. models and their mathematical models. And thus, I would like to conclude my *'pūrvapakṣa'* of the subject. In the next chapter, we shall commence our discussion about *'intelligence'*.

The brain and its complexity

Science is a differential equation. Religion is a boundary condition. – Alan Turing.

> *As you are reading this book, either holding it as a paperback or on your screen with your fingers scrolling, you are engaging your skin. If you like reading with some light background music, you will hear it through your ears. In case you are feeling dizzy, what could be better than a cup of coffee, with its smell being recognized by your nose and taste being validated by your tongue? Yet, if the content of the book is interesting enough, your eyes will pay attention to the words, not the fonts. Even though you would be sipping coffee or there is some background music, your utmost attention would be drawn towards contemplating the text you are reading. You will not be drawn away by your senses!*

Having concluded our investigation of the A.I. models, it would only be apt that we go forward and investigate the inspiration behind: *The Human Brain.*

But to what extent should this investigation lead? Even 5000 pages would not be sufficient to present the mysteries of the brain, and that kind of discussion is not in my scope as well, since I am a mere student at the entry level of this vast subject. It would then be wise to hold on to the established facts and build the narrative around them.

Since science rejects supernatural explanations for mental phenomena, Hippocrates (460–370 BCE), the father of Western medicine, argued that the brain is the seat of intelligence and sensation. The brain is a complex machine, comprising a network of ~86 billion neurons and trillions of synapses. It is perpetually active, even in the absence of environmental and body-derived stimuli. Here, when we say 'perpetually active', it means that most of the brain's activity is generated from within, and external stimulus only causes a minor perturbation from its robust state. When we add the complex adjective to a system, this usually applies to all the constituents the system is made of, and in the case of the brain, they would be *neurons*.

The brain is the seat of consciousness, but for our scientific exploration, we shall be putting off the philosophical lens for a bit. In regard to our current discussion, we shall simply be discussing how the brain processes information from external stimuli. Here, we are basically reducing the scope of the brain's capability to just process the input received, which stands in contrast to the artificial neurons we discussed in our previous lesson.

This simple and concise exploration is necessary to appreciate the complex nature of the human brain, especially at times when it is loosely compared with an entity that feeds on binary signals and presents an output.

Signal Processing in the Brain

Human beings are blessed with five special senses: olfaction (smell), gustation (taste), equilibrium (balance and body position), vision, and hearing, and additionally somatosensation, which deals with stimuli like temperature, pain, pressure, and vibration. Sensory input is one of the main functions of the Nervous system and is responsible for gathering data through sensory receptors and sending this information to the Central Nervous System (including the brain and spinal cord) via afferent sensory nerves. The vast network of sensory receptors forms the Peripheral Nervous System (PNS), which is further subdivided into the autonomic nervous system and the somatic nervous system. The autonomic system has involuntary control of internal organs, blood vessels, smooth and cardiac muscles. The somatic system has voluntary control of skin, bones, joints, and skeletal muscle.

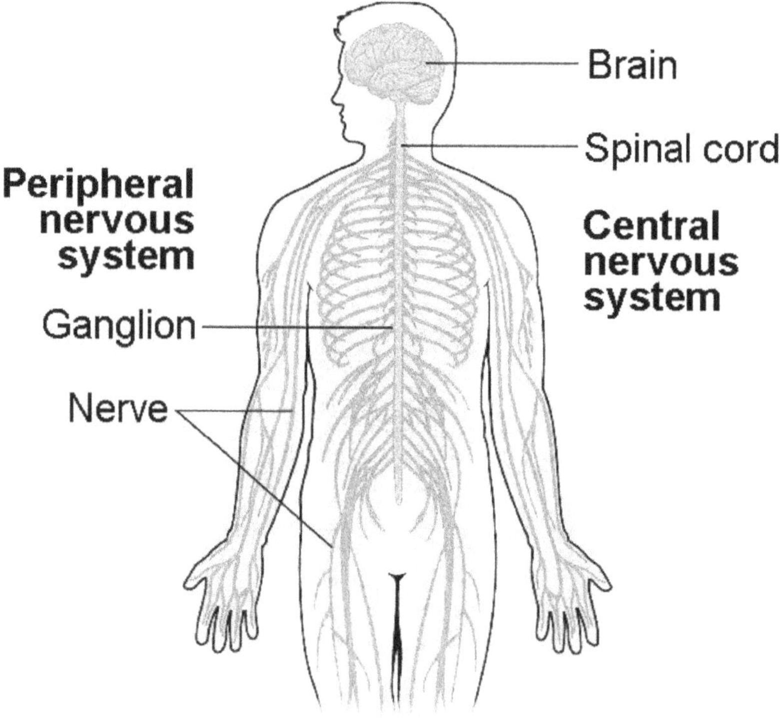

Figure 8 The Nervous System (source: lumenlearning.com)

Although the sensory systems associated with distinct senses are quite different, the most fundamental function of a sensory system is the translation of a sensory signal to an electrical signal in the nervous system. Understand that each of these organs has been assigned specific tasks, for example, the eyes are for vision, the ears for hearing, and so on. These organs merely pass on the information they collect to the human brain, which does the processing of the received information. But the brain does not process raw information such as images captured by our eyes or smells captured by our nose. It feeds on the electrical signals sent by the sensory receptor, which changes the sensory input, such as light, sound, or pressure, into a receptor potential.

To understand better, consider our skin, which serves as a protective barrier, a thermoregulator, and a sensory interface with the physical world. It is composed of multiple layers, each made up of various cell types, which work together to perform these functions. Central to this process are neurons, or nerve cells, specialized for transmitting information as electrical and chemical signals.

Neurons

Like all cells, a *neuron* is a tiny living unit enclosed by a cell membrane, a permeable layer that separates its inside (cytoplasm) from the outside environment. Inside the cell and in the fluids around it, there are ions (Na^+, K^+, Cl^-, etc.) with electric charge. The cell membrane is quite selective about allowing ions to pass through it. Even when the cell is idle, it has a difference in charge and ion concentration across its membrane. It keeps more sodium ions (Na$^+$) outside and more potassium ions (K$^+$) inside, a balance maintained by the sodium-potassium pump, which is a membrane protein that actively transports 3 Na$^+$ ions out of the cell and 2 K$^+$ ions in by using energy from ATP.

The cell membrane is more permeable to K$^+$ than to Na+. Hence, when K+ ions move out of the cell, they carry a positive charge, leaving behind a net negative charge on the inside of the cell, which is also contributed by the negatively charged proteins present within the cell.

STRUCTURE OF THE NEURON

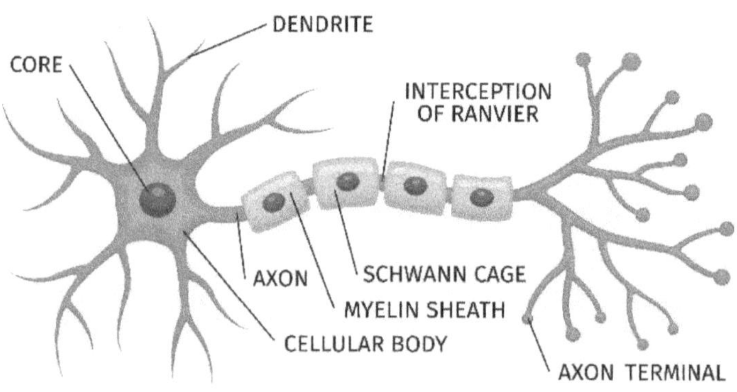

Figure 9 Structure of a neuron (Source: Wikimedia)

The structure of a neuron is uniquely adapted to its role in sensory signalling. A typical sensory neuron of several key components:

- **Cell Body (Soma):** The metabolic center of the neuron, containing the nucleus and organelles, is located in structures like the dorsal root ganglia near the spinal cord for sensory neurons. The soma integrates signals and supports the neuron's functions.
- **Dendrites:** These are branched extensions that are often extended into the skin as sensory endings to detect stimuli. These endings are where sensory transduction occurs, such as in mechanoreceptors.
- **Axon:** A long, slender projection that conducts electrical impulses (action potentials) from the sensory endings or cell body to the Central Nervous System (CNS). Sensory axons can be myelinated (covered with a fatty insulating layer called myelin) for rapid signal transmission or unmyelinated for slower conduction, depending on the type of sensation (e.g., touch vs. pain).
- **Axon Terminals:** These are the endpoints of the axon, which form synapses with other neurons in the spinal cord or brain, and release neurotransmitters to relay the sensory signal.
- **Nodes of Ranvier:** In myelinated axons, these are gaps in the myelin sheath where ion channels and sodium-potassium pumps are concentrated, which enable fast signal propagation via saltatory conduction.

The sodium-potassium pump operates in the plasma membrane across all these regions and maintains the ion gradients essential for the neuron's electrical properties. The dendritic endings in the skin often form *mechanoreceptors*, which are specialized sensory receptors that detect mechanical stimuli like touch or pressure. When a stimulus like a pinch occurs, the mechanoreceptor's membrane is well equipped to translate this mechanical input into an electrical signal by leveraging the polarized state of the neuron.

External Stimuli

When we are at rest, a neuron has a membrane potential of approximately -70 mV, maintained by the sodium-potassium pump and the selective permeability of the membrane. If there is a pinch on the skin, the skin is physically deformed, and it causes the Na+ channels in the Mechanoreceptors to enter and make the inside of the cell less negative. The cell may depolarize from -70 mV to -60 mV or more, depending on the intensity of the pinch. This shift in the membrane potential is called receptor potential, a graded potential that reflects the strength of the stimulus. If the receptor potential is strong enough to reach the threshold (typically -55 to -50 mV), it triggers an action potential by mechanically opening voltage-gated Na^+ channels, usually at the axon hillock or the first node of Ranvier. The action potential then propagates along the axon all the way to the CNS, where it may lead to the release of neurotransmitters at the axon terminals and relay the sensory signal to other neurons.

Like a line of falling dominoes or a ripple in the surface of the water, the action potential propagates along the axon. Unlike a passive electrical signal that weakens with distance, the action potential is actively regenerated at each segment of the axon, and thus maintains its amplitude and strength. The electrical disturbance (depolarization) triggers a new, identical disturbance in the next segment, and thus creates a continuous or jumping wave depending on whether the axon is unmyelinated or myelinated.

When an action potential lands at one segment of the axon (e.g., near the axon hillock or the first node of Ranvier), the rapid influx of Na^+ through voltage-gated Na^+ channels makes the inside of the membrane positive (+30 mV). This creates a local current as positive charges (primarily Na^+ ions) flow toward adjacent, more negative regions of the axon that are still at the resting potential (-70 mV) and depolarize the neighbouring membrane segment. This process repeats along the axon, with each segment generating its action potential as the depolarization wave advances.

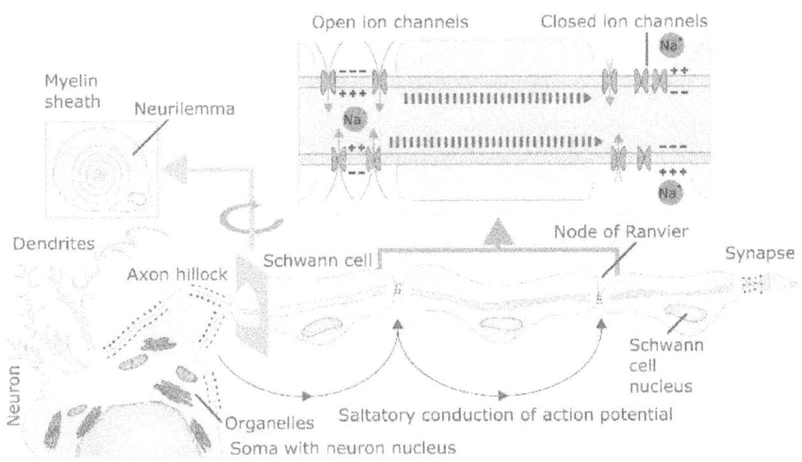

Figure 10 Schematic representation of the action potential propagation through a myelinated nerve fiber of the peripheral nervous system. Source: Wikimedia

After an action potential, the membrane enters a refractory period, during which Na$^+$ channels become inactivated and cannot reopen, and voltage-gated K$^+$ channels open, allowing K$^+$ to exit and repolarize the membrane back toward -70 mV. This refractory period ensures that the wave moves unidirectionally toward the axon terminal without retracing its path.

In unmyelinated axons (e.g., C fibers for pain or temperature), the flow of charges is continuous but slower (0.5–2 m/s), with every segment of the axon membrane undergoing an action potential. In myelinated axons (e.g., A-beta fibers for touch, common in mechanoreceptors for pressure), charges flow in a jumping fashion, known as saltatory conduction. The myelin sheath, formed by Schwann cells, insulates the axon and prevents ion flow except at the nodes of Ranvier, where voltage-gated Na$^+$ channels and sodium-potassium pumps are concentrated. When an action potential occurs at one node, the local current jumps to the next node and triggers a new action potential. This creates a wave that appears to leap from node to node, significantly increasing the speed of propagation (up to 100–120 m/s).

Role of the Central Nervous System

Once the action potential reaches the axon terminals in the Central Nervous System (CNS), neurotransmitters are triggered, and they transmit the sensory signal to second-order neurons in sensory pathways. The second-order neurons are interneurons located in either the spinal cord or the brainstem, and they relay the information signal received to the thalamus or cerebellum. But these are not the only signals converging on the brain at any given moment. The skin alone contains thousands of sensory neurons, and other sensory systems (vision, hearing, etc.) add to this barrage of information. Now the onus is on the brain to filter out irrelevant signals, distinguish between different inputs, and prioritize those that demand attention.

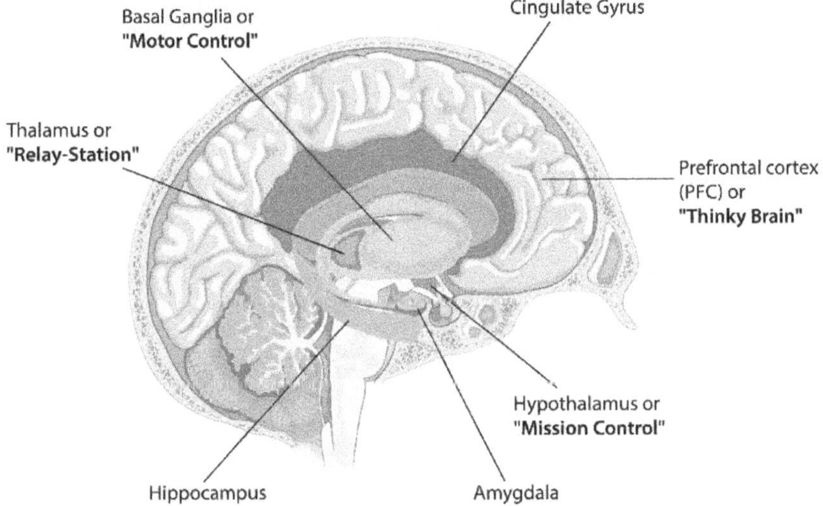

Figure 11 Brain cross-section with sub-cortical structures (source: Physiopedia)

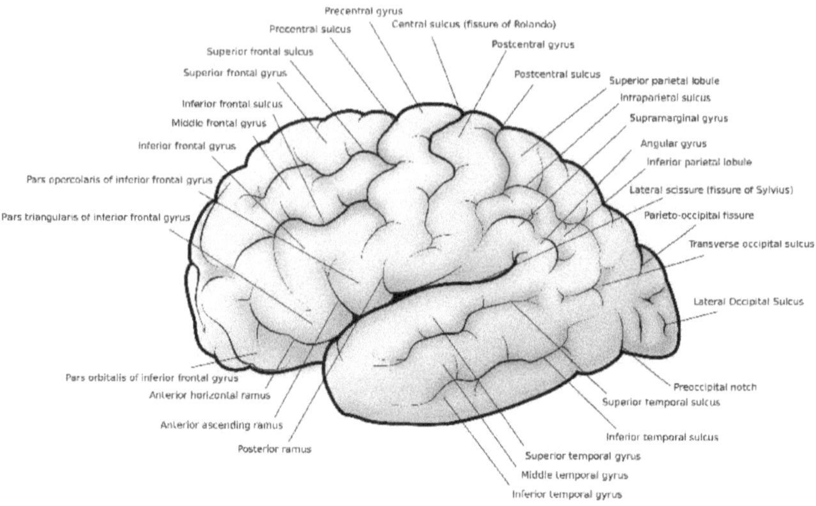

Figure 12 Cerebral Cortex (source: Wikipedia)

Complex behaviors, such as distinguishing a ball from a book using only touch, involve the coordinated activity of multiple brain regions, including both subcortical structures and cortical areas. Subcortical structures are a group of diverse neural formations deep within the brain, which include the diencephalon, pituitary gland, limbic structures, and the basal ganglia. They are the information hubs of the CNS, as they relay and modulate information to different areas of the brain. They are actively involved in complex activities such as memory, emotion, pleasure, and hormone production.

The cortical area, primarily the cerebral cortex, is a dense layer of neuronal cell bodies that form the outer layer of the brain and completely covers the surface of the two cerebral hemispheres. Due to its larger surface area, it has a comparatively higher number of neurons within it and hence has a broad range of functions, including perception and awareness of sensory information, planning, and initiation of motor activity. It also plays a key role in higher cognitive functions, such as decision making, motivation, attention, learning, memory, problem-solving, and conceptual thinking.

Information Processing

In the brain, sensory information is processed in a hierarchical manner: the signal travels through multiple processing stages, from lower (subcortical) to higher (cortical) centers. At each level, the information becomes more detailed and refined. Even within a single sensory system, such as touch, different aspects of the stimulus are handled by separate neural pathways. For example, in the somatosensory system, a light touch and a painful pinprick to the same area of skin are detected and processed by distinct neural circuits, each specialized for different types of sensory input. The action potential from a mechanoreceptor detecting a pinch may travel via myelinated A-beta fibers to the spinal cord and then to the thalamus (a subcortical relay station) before reaching the primary somatosensory cortex (S1), where the sensation is consciously perceived. On the contrary, a painful pinprick may involve slower, unmyelinated C fibers, processed through different spinal and cortical pathways. So, we have a barrage of information coming to our brain via various pathways, originating from various receptors.

But we do not react to every change in the environment around us. For example, while playing video games for long hours, one may not even notice what is going on around or even one's own needs, such as the need for a water break or giving rest to the eyes. This is because we chose to focus on the heightened sensation at a particular moment while ignoring irrelevant or redundant information. Understand, the natural tendency of the system is to conserve as much energy as possible. Hence, the nervous system starts filtering the stimuli at the level of sensory receptors (part of the PNS) only, which reduces the amount of sensory data fed to the CNS. This entry level of filtering is called Peripheral filtering. For example, Photoreceptors in the retina (rods and cones) absorb light within certain wavelengths but filter out non-visual stimuli. Sensory receptors adapt to sustained or repetitive stimuli so that constant or predictable inputs are filtered out. For example, in the auditory system, hair cells adapt to continuous sounds but remain responsive to new auditory events. Now you know, while watching a horror movie, sound effects matter!

The PNS passes on the relevant information to the CNS, where the subcortical region is the first landing point of the data. In the subcortical region, the thalamus serves as a central relay and filtering station for sensory information. Based on behavioral state, attention, and context, the thalamus does filtration. For example, when we are awake, neurons in the thalamus fire steadily to transmit sensory inputs to the cortex; however, while sleeping, there is a rhythmic burst of neurons that reduces sensory throughput.

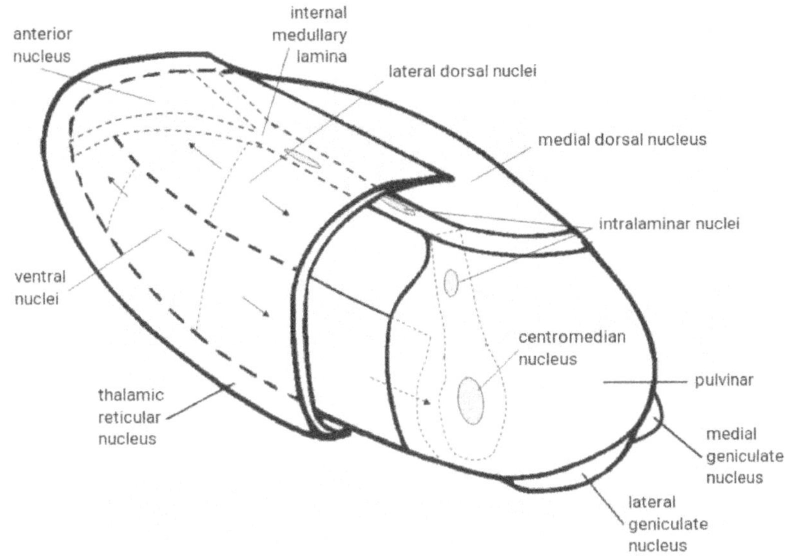

Figure 13 The part of the Thalamus

Sensory information is relayed through specific thalamic nuclei. For example, Ventral Posterior Lateral (VPL) Nucleus processes somatosensory inputs (touch, pressure, pain) from the body via the dorsal column-medial lemniscus and spinothalamic tracts. Lateral Geniculate Nucleus (LGN) relays visual inputs from the retina via the optic nerve. The Medial Geniculate Nucleus (MGN) handles auditory inputs from the cochlea via the auditory nerve. The thalamic reticular nucleus (TRN), a thin sheet of GABAergic neurons surrounding the thalamus, acts as a filter by inhibiting irrelevant or excessive sensory inputs. These nuclei receive sensory inputs, process them, and project to primary sensory cortices.

Filtering

The brain does not just filter out information but also distinguishes between multiple simultaneous signals through parallel processing, topographic organization, and neural oscillations. As we mentioned earlier, in the somatosensory system, touch (via A-beta fibers) and pain (via C fibers) travel through separate pathways, which ensures that a pinch's pressure and a pinprick's pain are processed independently, even if they occur at the same skin location. Apart from that, the brain has a topological map of different body regions, so that it can distinguish the location of each signal via its specific neurons.

Certain neurons, particularly in the thalamus and cortex, exhibit intrinsic rhythmicity due to the presence of specific ion channels. For example, T-type Ca^{2+} Channels, found in neurons at the ventral posterior lateral nucleus (VPL) and thalamic reticular nucleus (TRN) areas, activate at hyperpolarized potentials (~-70 mV). Ion channels are specialized proteins embedded in cell membranes that act as pathways for ions to cross the membrane. These ion channels are "gated"; basically, they can open and close in response to specific stimuli. When the membrane potential becomes very negative (hyperpolarized), T-type Ca^{2+} channels are ready to open. Once the membrane depolarizes, channel gates are open and Ca^{2+} ions rush into the cell, which triggers a low-threshold calcium spike (LTS). As the membrane depolarizes and crosses the threshold of voltage-gated Na^+ channels, there is a fast inward sodium current. Since LTS lasts tens of milliseconds, the membrane stays depolarized for a while, and as a result, there are multiple fast Na^+ dependent action potentials firing on top of LTS.

During low arousal states, this rhythmic firing (burst of action potential) occurs at a 4–8 Hz frequency range (theta) or 8–12 Hz frequency range (alpha). Likewise, in cortical pyramidal neurons, Na^+ triggers rhythmic firing in the 30–100 Hz frequency range (gamma) during high arousal states such as attention, feature binding, and sensory integration.

Synaptic Transmission

Now, neurons are either excitatory or inhibitory. Excitatory neurons, for example, pyramidal neurons, found in the cortex (~80% of neurons in the cortex), release glutamate (a type of neurotransmitter) upon firing. These neurons often have long axons to project signals across brain regions and dendrites with spines, due to which they receive many synaptic inputs. Glutamate binds to postsynaptic receptors (at the end of synapses) like AMPA receptors and NMDA receptors, which causes positive ions (e.g., Na^+, Ca^{2+}) to enter the postsynaptic neuron. As a result, depolarization occurs, and neurons are most likely to fire. This state is called an excitatory postsynaptic potential (EPSP).

Synaptic Transmission

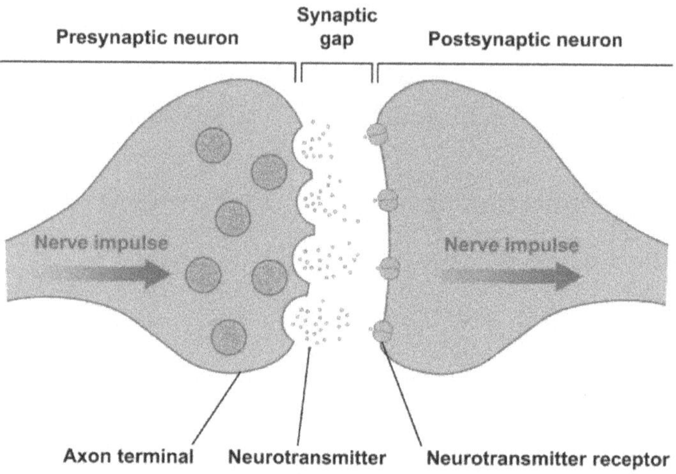

Figure 14 Synaptic Transmission (source: www.simplypsychology.org)

Inhibitory neurons (for example: Interneurons in the cortex, hippocampus, and other regions) release GABA (gamma-aminobutyric acid, a type of neurotransmitter) that decrease the likelihood of the postsynaptic neuron firing an action potential by hyperpolarizing its membrane (moving the membrane potential further from the firing threshold) or by stabilizing it. In contrast with excitatory neurons, these neurons typically have short axons and lack dendritic spines. In the synaptic cleft, when GABA binds to postsynaptic receptors (for example, GABA_A, GABA_B), ions such as Cl^-, K^+, etc. exit the neuron, leaving it hyperpolarized. This state is called inhibitory postsynaptic potential (IPSP).

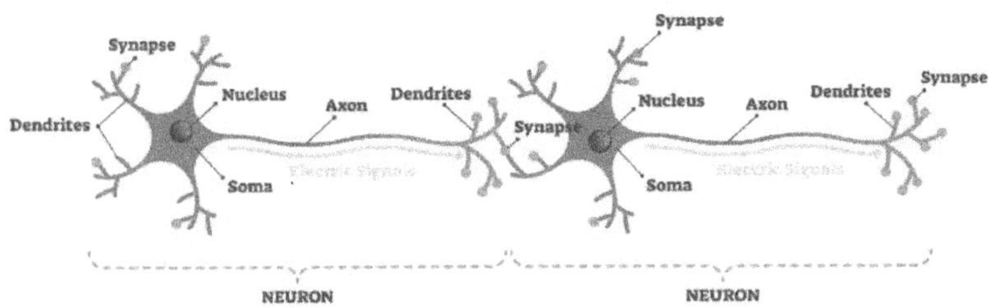

Figure 15 Synaptic Transmission (source: www.simplypsychology.org)

Excitatory and inhibitory neurons work together to balance neural activity, which ensures that our brain is neither overexcited nor overly suppressed. Together, they form an Excitatory-Inhibitory Feedback Loop. For example, When A pyramidal neuron fires, it releases glutamate onto a PV interneuron, which triggers the interneuron to fire. In response, the PV interneuron releases GABA onto the pyramidal neuron, temporarily inhibiting it. Once the inhibition wears off, usually in ~5–10 milliseconds (due to the fast decay of GABA_A IPSPs), the pyramidal neuron can fire again.

Brain Oscillation Patterns

The Excitatory-Inhibitory Feedback Loop creates a rhythmic alternation of excitation and inhibition that spreads across the dense network between pyramidal cells and interneurons within a cortical region and synchronizes their firing into a coherent network oscillation. The frequency of the network oscillation (e.g., gamma, theta, delta) is determined by the interplay of intrinsic neuronal properties, synaptic kinetics, and network dynamics. For example, the fast kinetics of

There Is No A.I.

GABA_A (decay ~5–10 ms) and AMPA receptors, combined with the rapid spiking of PV interneurons, result in oscillation cycles (gamma) every 10–25 ms (40–100 Hz).

To coordinate and separate sensory signals to support higher-order functions like attention, memory, and perception, the brain uses oscillatory rhythms. Neural

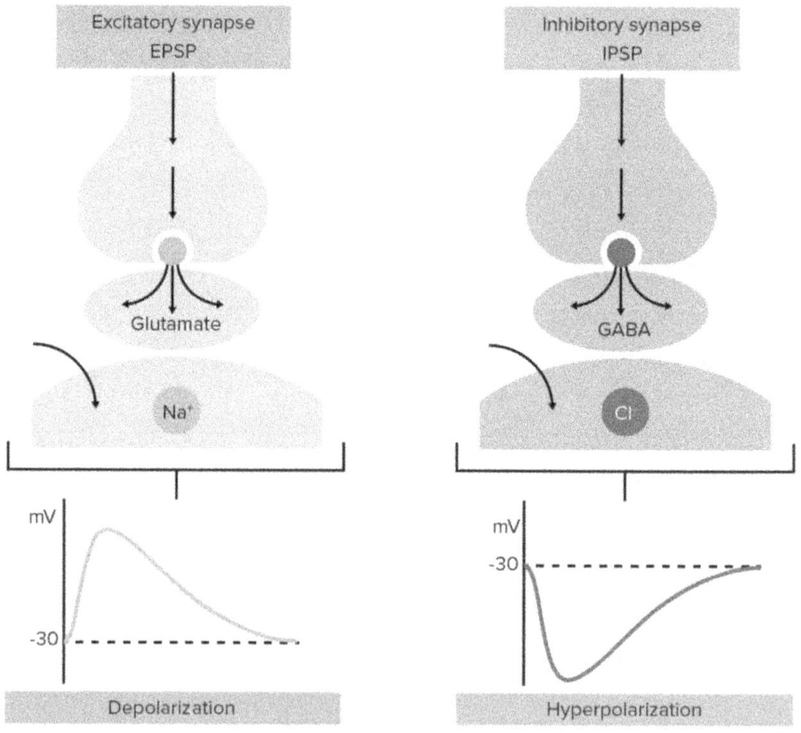

Figure 16 Excitatory-Inhibitory Feedback Loop (source: www.lecturio.com)

Oscillations can be measured by EEG and MEG devices, with Fourier Transform-based spectral analysis, revealing their frequency content, which can be mapped to sensory processing during different activities. Some key frequency bands and their mapping with related activities are provided in the table below.

Frequency Band	Range (Hz)	Main Activities	Primary Brain Regions
Delta	0.5–4	Deep sleep, healing, restorative processes	Thalamus, cortex (during sleep)
Theta	4–8	Attention, memory encoding, and sensory integration	Hippocampus, prefrontal cortex
Alpha	8–12	Relaxed wakefulness, inhibition of irrelevant sensory input	Occipital cortex, parietal areas
Beta	13–30	Sensorimotor activities, alertness, and maintaining active tasks	Sensorimotor cortex, frontal regions
Gamma	30–100	Attention, feature binding, complex sensory integration	Visual cortex, associative cortical areas

Neural oscillations create temporal windows of excitability, during which neurons are more or less responsive to incoming signals. This compartmentalization helps the brain to segregate inputs from different sources in distinct time windows, bind related sensory features into coherent percepts, and amplify relevant signals and suppress irrelevant ones. For example, when a pinch stimulates Pacinian corpuscles, action potentials reach S1 via the Ventral posterolateral nucleus (VPL). Gamma oscillations synchronize S1 neurons and enhance the representation of the pinch's vibration (50–300 Hz) and location. At the same time, alpha oscillations increase in S1 regions representing other body parts, such as arms, which blocks the less important sensory signals from the arm. This ensures that the pinch is perceived clearly, even though other skin areas are simultaneously stimulated.

Non-Linearity of the Brain

Information can be constantly exchanged across boundaries, as evident in complex systems. In the case of the brain, this is done through the dense neural circuits. The evolution of such a complex system as the brain is characterized by *nonlinear differential equations*, because they exchange energy with the surrounding environment (e.g., via sensory input and metabolic processes) and lose energy over time. It is the energy dissipation that drives a dynamic process like neuronal communication. We call these systems *Dissipative Systems*, as suggested by the Belgian-American chemist Ilya Prigogine.

Nonlinearity arises because neuronal interactions are not additive. A small change in input (e.g., slight variations in light or brain state) can lead to disproportionate changes in activity due to feedback loops, inhibition, and excitation. Past experiences modify synaptic connections (via Hebbian learning or long-term potentiation). The system itself is chaotic. As Gyorgy Buzsaki subtly puts it in his book The Rhythms of the Brain, "*The spatiotemporal trajectory of neuronal activity depends not only on the constellation of light impinging on the retina but also on the perceiver's brain state and experience with similar physical inputs".*

In a periodic system, to predict the future, we need a model that truly reflects the past. However, causality among world events is linked to our perception of time. According to Walter J. Freeman, time exists in the material world as a measure of motion, applicable to both living and non-living entities, yet he also argues that causality is a construct of human intentionality. Predictions and relationships are constructed by the successful ordering of the events according to elapsed subjective time. As time progresses, precision decreases. Let us consider the illustration where the brain exhibits *"logical illusion"*:

"You are driving on a highway, and you suddenly spot a dog crossing the road. You instantly press the brake pedal and the car halts."

If you are asked to mentally reconstruct what happened earlier, you (considering you are not a neuroscientist) will most likely say that you noticed a dog (cause) and realized your car would hit the animal fatally and hence applied the brakes (effect). However, in a laboratory setting, the explanation would be as follows: a dog appeared on the road (first event), the driver applied the brake (second event), and the driver recognized the animal as a dog (third event).

So, what happened exactly?

Our brain reacts to an unexpected event (less than half a second) faster than it consciously recognizes an object (longer than half a second). Conscious recognition involves dense and distributed neural circuits, where information is broadcast across multiple brain regions. Within 200–300 ms, the brain may extract features like "four legs" or "brown color" in the inferotemporal cortex. However, full conscious recognition ("It is a dog, and it will be dangerous to hit it") requires integrating these features with memory (hippocampus), context (prefrontal cortex), and attention (parietal cortex), which takes over 500 ms. The synchronization takes time, as it requires coordinating millions of neurons across the cortex. During this time, unconscious reflexes (e.g., braking) can occur, as they rely on faster, simpler circuits.

However, during mental reconstruction of the event, the brain integrates sensory, motor, and cognitive information into a coherent percept, as if it is trying to compensate for the delay. So, what do we conclude from the above illustration?

"Our time reconstruction is a consequence of an accumulation of past experience rather than a truthful representation of real time". - Gyorgy Buzsaki.

What Buzsaki suggests is that even if the same stimulus is presented multiple times, the neuronal trajectory is unique due to the brain's nonlinear dynamics. He further suggests that complexity can be perceived as non-linearity, and from non-linear equations, unexpected solutions emerge. The reason is that it is not easy to predict the dynamic behavior of a complex system or even that it cannot be deduced from the behavior of lower-level entities (constituents the system is made of), as they are themselves complex in nature and independent at many levels.

But independence of constituents at many levels does not mean that the behavior of a system is defined by the sum of local interactions. The emerging behavior of a complex system at one point in time is determined from the manifold interactions of various constituents of the system, and even a slight change can significantly change the resultant behavior of the system.

End Note

Now that we have come to terms with the complex nature of the brain and understand the science behind one of the core activities it performs, we are ready to explore the mathematical models of the functioning of such a system.

Mathematical Models of the Brain

If a 'religion' is defined to be a system of ideas that contains unprovable statements, then Gödel taught us that mathematics is not only a religion, it is the only religion that can prove itself to be one. - John D. Barrow

Science is the journey of discovering the laws behind an observation. It starts with an observation and searches for a domain where the observation becomes a fact. Then it searches for the rules in the domain and the connected domains. Ultimately, it must find a path from the connected planes to the law. In this ever-changing world, there may exist an infinite number of paths with their permutations and combinations, going through infinite possible planes. Hence, tying a single observation to a law is not possible.

The laws are unbending. For example: Law is not how Societies and their people "should" function, but it is the way humans and Societies "would" function, regardless. And science is the tool that tries to model this complexity. But how do we represent this complexity?

Johannes Kepler says, *"The chief aim of all investigations of the external world should be to discover the rational order and harmony which has been imposed on it by God and which He revealed to us in the language of mathematics."*

In the last chapter, we came to terms with the fact that the brain is an adaptive complex system. And such a system is quite hard to predict. For instance, when light hits the retina, it triggers a cascade of neuronal activity from the retina to higher brain regions (e.g., visual cortex, memory systems). This activity can be modelled as a trajectory in a multidimensional state space, where each dimension corresponds to the activity of specific neurons or brain regions. But this trajectory is not fixed and depends on various factors but primarily the external stimulus (in this case, it will be pattern of light), the brain's internal state (is it attentive or in a good or bad mood) and experience (brain functions on associative memory, i.e., neurons that fire together, wire together). This means that the same stimulus can produce a different trajectory each time, and this fact underlines the brain's adaptability and individuality.

In physics, such systems are called *open systems*. They interact with their environment and exchange energy with their surroundings. They are dynamic and ever evolving. Natural phenomena such as living organisms, avalanches, earthquakes, etc., are dynamic open systems. They exhibit complex behaviors such as self-organization, where patterns or structures emerge spontaneously. Belgian scientist Viscount Ilya Romanovich Prigogine introduced the term *"dissipative structures"* for these organized patterns that occur in open systems far from equilibrium.

The state of 'far from equilibrium' means the system in this state is either driven by external inputs or internal instabilities. They cannot settle into a stable, predictable state, which can be described by linear equations.

Classical thermodynamics fails to explain their behavior. Prigogine suggested that in open systems which are far from equilibrium, second law of thermodynamics holds globally (total entropy of system and surrounding increases) but local order can emerge within the system since the system exports its entropy to its environment and its entropy decreases in this process, as a result organized structures are formed. Take metabolic processes, for example, where the system consumes energy-rich molecules (glucose) and reduces lower energy waste.

Consider our brain, which is perpetually active, even in the absence of environmental and body-derived stimuli. (Buzsaki 2006). As a matter of fact, perturbation from an external stimulus causes only a slight deviation from its original robust state. Nonetheless, these external disturbances are crucial for adapting the brain's internal operations to perform real-world functions. The brain has to be calibrated to the metrics of the environment it lives in, and its internal connections should be modified accordingly. This calibration happens as a result of its interaction with its surroundings, mostly other 'brains' (humans). And this stands true at the cellular level as well.

Since such open dynamic systems cannot be modelled using linear mathematics, as there is no proportional relationship, the only way to model such systems is through non-linear differential equations. These equations do not have universal solutions, and a small change in initial conditions can lead to drastically different outcomes.

But what are Differential Equations?

Many of the principles, or laws, underlying the behavior of the natural world are statements or relations involving rates at which things happen. When expressed in mathematical terms, the *"relations are equations"*, and the *"rates are derivatives"*. And equations containing derivatives are *differential equations*. Therefore, to understand and investigate problems involving motion of fluids, current, heat, or seismic waves, etc., certain familiarity with differential equations is required. A differential equation that describes some physical process is called a *mathematical model* of the process. (William E. Boyce 2005). In essence, they describe the evolution of systems in continuous time.

We are not new to dynamic phenomena; it is just that we are currently paying attention to the modelling of such processes. A process as normal as a free-falling object can be modelled through differential equations. We represent force F acting on an object of mass m with certain acceleration a, which is the rate of change of velocity v concerning time t as:

$$F = ma = m\frac{dv}{dt} \tag{1}$$

In the case of a free-falling object, gravity and air resistance will act upon the object as it falls. Gravity g will be pulling the object downwards and is more prominent here, and air resistance will be dragging the object in the upward direction. The drag due to air resistance will be difficult to model, and hence we assume that the drag is proportional to the velocity v of the object. Thus, the drag of air resistance will have a magnitude of $\gamma . v$, where γ is a constant called the drag coefficient. Since both gravity and air resistance are acting in opposite directions, we will represent the net force F acting on a free-falling object as:

$$F = mg - \gamma v \tag{2}$$

Taking a cue from Eq. (1), we can rewrite the above equation as:

$$m\frac{dv}{dt} = mg - \gamma v \tag{3}$$

For the sake of simplification, we can divide out the mass m:

$$\frac{dv}{dt} = g - \frac{\gamma v}{m} \tag{4}$$

The equation (4) we have now is a first-order linear differential equation, which, upon solving, will give the velocity v of a falling object of mass m that has both gravity and air resistance acting upon it. To solve the above equation, we need to find a function $v = v(t)$.

Assuming certain values for the quantities in the equation above, say mass is 2 kg, and $\gamma = 0.392$, The equation can be written as:

$$\frac{dv}{dt} = 9.8 - 0.196v \tag{5}$$

The above equation tells us how velocity v changes with respect to time t. Rather than solving it analytically, we can investigate the behavior of the solution from a geometrical viewpoint. For instance, if value $v=0$ at some point, then $\frac{dv}{dt} = 9.8$. This suggests that the velocity is increasing rapidly. Now, suppose at some point t, velocity v is 30, which means $\frac{dv}{dt} = 3.92$. The change in velocity is still positive, which suggests that the velocity of the object is still increasing, but slowly. But, if we substitute values like this in the equation, we can see a trend that as velocity v increases, $\frac{dv}{dt}$ decreases. Now, if we visualize this behavior on a grid plane by plotting small arrows (slopes) at points (t, v), we will get a direction field plot indicating the direction in which a solution curve would proceed from that point.

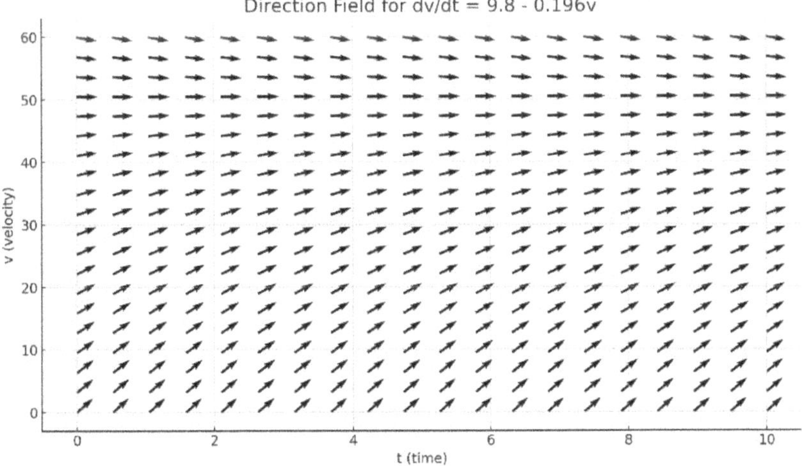

Since the arrows in the direction field represent the slopes (tangents) of solution curves, we can follow the arrows to sketch the paths that solutions take. The direction field plot above shows all solutions flattening out and approaching $v = 50$ over time. This is a classic example of exponential decay toward equilibrium.

Visualizing a solution via a direction field is quite useful, especially in the case of non-linear differential equations, where finding an analytical solution is difficult or impossible. Rather than labouring to solve the actual equation, we get the big picture of the system dynamics, the focus of our study. Direction fields reveal how solutions behave as time increases, which is often more important than the exact solution. Now that we have an idea about what differential equations are, we are ready to study mathematical models representing neuronal communications, and the Hodgkin-Huxley Model should be a good place to start.

Modelling a Neuron

Alan Hodgkin and Andrew Huxley met in 1938 at Trinity College, Cambridge, where Huxley was an undergraduate student, and Hodgkin was a teacher. Both were interested in understanding the particular dynamics of ion flow in neurons, so they began to conduct their research as partners at the Plymouth Marine Laboratory in 1939.

> ### *Quick Recap about Neurons, which we studied in Chapter 2*
>
> Like all cells, a *neuron* is a tiny living unit enclosed by a cell membrane, a permeable layer that separates its inside (cytoplasm) from the outside environment. Inside the cell and in the fluids around it, there are ions (Na+, K^+, Cl^-, etc.) with electric charge. The cell membrane is quite selective about allowing ions to pass through it. Even when the cell is idle, it has a difference in charge and ion concentration across its membrane. It keeps more sodium ions (Na+) outside and more potassium ions (K^+) inside, a balance maintained

by the sodium-potassium pump, which is a membrane protein that actively transports 3 Na^+ ions out of the cell and 2 K^+ ions in by using energy from ATP.

The cell membrane is more permeable to K^+ than to Na+. Hence, when K+ ions move out of the cell, they carry a positive charge, leaving behind a net negative charge on the inside of the cell, which is also contributed by the negatively charged proteins present within the cell.

In the 1930s and 1940s, neuroscientists were beginning to explore the mechanisms of nerve impulse transmission. The prevailing question was how neurons generate and propagate electrical signals, known as action potentials (refer to chapter 2). Early work by researchers like Kenneth Cole and Howard Curtis suggested that action potentials involved changes in membrane conductance by the movement of sodium ions across the neuronal membrane through proteins called ion channels, but the precise mechanisms were unclear. One of the difficulties in understanding action potentials was that neurons are incredibly small. At their largest, they are about 100 mm, but they can be under 10 mm. By comparison, a human hair is about 80 mm. Scientists found that the size of the axons in most species made it difficult or impossible to insert a recording device to measure voltage changes during an action potential. Alan Hodgkin and Andrew Huxley got around this problem by studying action potentials in the relatively enormous axons of the squid.

The Hodgkin-Huxley model

Squid can jet rapidly by contracting muscles in their mantle cavity, expelling water through a siphon on the underside of their body. This action is initiated by the giant axon. Since squid do not have a skull to constrain the growth of their neurons, this axon can measure up to 1.5 mm in diameter. Its large size means that its signal propagates extremely quickly, allowing the squid to rapidly respond to danger. The giant squid axon, with its large diameter, offered a unique opportunity for precise electrophysiological measurements.

Figure 17 A Squid, via Wikipedia, licensed under CC BY-SA 4.0.

The giant axon is hundreds of times larger than the largest axons in humans, making it much easier to study; moreover, it is visible to the naked eye, and it is possible to insert the tip of a microelectrode into the membrane to record its activity. Hodgkin and Huxley took advantage of this fact to interrogate the electrochemical dynamics of neurons with the help of the voltage clamp technique, pioneered by Kenneth Cole and George Marmont. (Schwiening 2012).

In this process, the giant axon was submerged in a solution of ions. Two wires were inserted into the membrane, and another was inserted into the solution. The two wires inside and outside the cell recorded the voltage, and the difference between these values represented the membrane potential. The third electrode was used to stimulate the neuron with varying amounts of current and record the corresponding changes in voltage. The voltage clamp let them pause the voltage at different levels (e.g., -60 mV, 0 mV) and watch how sodium and potassium ions flowed.

Through the experiment, it was discovered that the membrane potential of the neuron reversed during an action potential, causing the neuron to momentarily have a positive membrane potential. This rapid reversal of membrane potential was the impetus for the generation of the electrical signal underlying the action potential. Scientists discovered that Sodium ions (Na^+) rush into the neuron when the voltage rises, which causes the action potential's sharp spike; and Potassium ions (K^+) flow out more slowly, which helps the voltage return to its resting state. And the flow of the current through the cell membrane was controlled by specific voltage-dependent ion channels, one for Sodium and another for Potassium. This reciprocal interaction between voltage and conductance allows positive and negative feedback loops with extremely rapid kinetics.

Unfortunately, Hodgkin and Huxley took their first recordings in 1939, just weeks before Hitler invaded Poland, marking the start of World War II. Their research was postponed for seven years, but they were eventually able to continue their work and develop their beautiful set of equations (using only a hand-operated calculator) that attempt to describe the biological mechanisms of neuronal firing (Juliet Bockhorst n.d.).

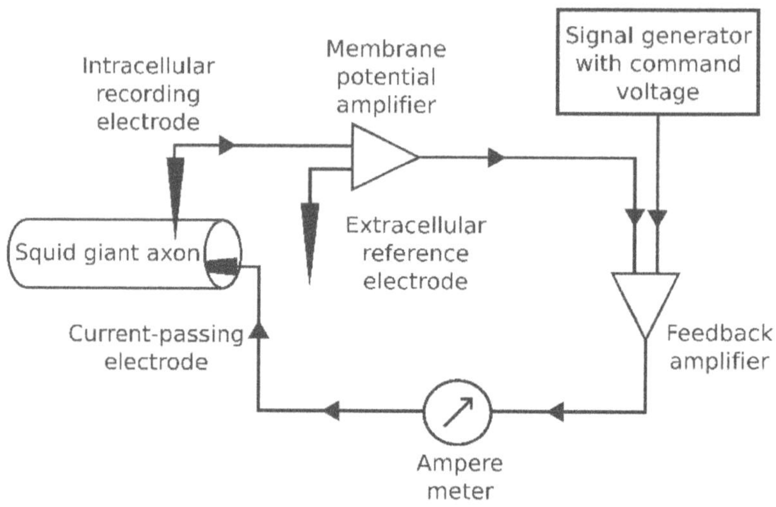

Figure 18 Voltage Clamp Setup demonstration, via Wikipedia, licensed under CC BY-SA 4.0.

Hodgkin and Huxley wanted to create a mathematical model to explain and predict action potentials. They imagined the neuron's membrane as an electrical circuit, like a tiny battery with wires and switches. In this model, the membrane acts like a capacitor that stores electrical charge. When ions move, the voltage changes, like charging or discharging a battery. This process can be represented by the following equation:

$$C_m \frac{dV}{dt} = I - I_{ion}$$

Here, C_m is the membrane's capacitance, (V) is the voltage, (I) is any external current (like from an electrode), and

I_{ion} is the current from ions moving through the membrane. This ionic current I_{ion} comes from three sources, Sodium (making the inside more positive), Potassium (making the inside more negative), and leak current (A small, constant flow of other ions like chloride through the membrane) (Izhikevich 2007).

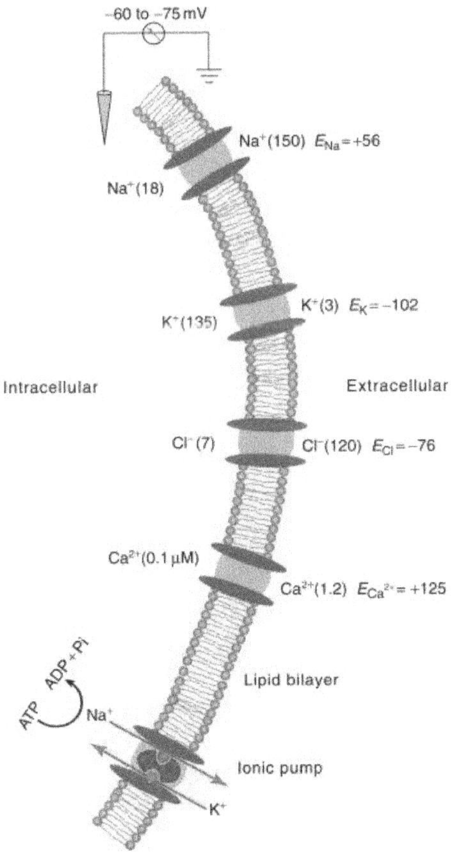

Figure 19: Differential distribution of ions inside and outside the plasma membrane of neurons and neuronal processes. Source:

There Is No A.I.

https://www.sciencedirect.com/topics/immunology-and-microbiology/nerve-cell-membrane-potential

The equation for ionic current was written as:

$$I_{ion} = g_{Na}(v - E_{Na}) + g_k(v - E_k) + g_L(v - E_L)$$

Here, g_{Na}, g_k and g_L are the conductance and E_{Na}, E_K and E_L are the reversal potentials (the voltages where each ion's flow balances out). The values of conductance variables changed with voltage and time, as ion channels opened and closed. To describe this behavior, Hodgkin and Huxley invented *gating variables*. The hypothesis was that the gates behave like a two-state system. Sodium channels were attributed two gates, namely Activation (*m, represented by sodium getting in*) and Inactivation (*h, represented by stopping sodium flow*). Potassium channels had one gate for Activation (n) only.

While doing the experiment, Hodgkin and Huxley found that potassium currents turned on slowly when the voltage increased (depolarization) and turned off when the voltage decreased. Unlike sodium currents, which turned off even if the voltage stayed high (inactivation), potassium currents stayed on as long as the voltage was high. This suggests that potassium channels don't have an inactivation process, and hence only one gate for activation.

Let us consider the sodium activation gate (*m*). Its value would change as follows:

> ➢ If m = 1, all gates are open.

There Is No A.I.

> If m = 0, all gates are closed.
> If m = 0.5, on average, half the gates are open.

And the rate of change $\frac{dm}{dt}$ of these gates with respect to time t was represented by the following differential equation:

$$\frac{dm}{dt} = (rate\ of\ opening) - (rate\ of\ closing)$$

$$\frac{dm}{dt} = \alpha_m(1 - m) - \beta_m m$$

Here, α_m and β_m are rates that depend on voltage. The equation is conveying the message that the probability of gates being open increases when more gates are open and decreases when more gates are closed. Hodgkin and Huxley didn't just guess the form of the equation but derived it from their voltage clamp data. They stepped the membrane voltage to various levels (e.g., from -70 mV to 0 mV) and recorded sodium and potassium currents, and then separated the currents by changing the bath solution. They calculated conductance (how easily ions flow) from the currents using Ohm's law and observed that conductance rose and fell with specific time courses. For example, potassium conductance increased slowly, suggesting a slow activation gate. (Hodgkin n.d.).

This set of equations represents the Hodgkin-Huxley model, which explains how neurons communicate. They either fire fully or not at all, depending on whether the voltage crosses a threshold. It was the first detailed explanation of how neurons work electrically and helped scientists understand brain disorders (like epilepsy, caused by faulty ion channels), design drugs, and build computer models of the brain. This model was further simplified by the FitzHugh-Nagumo model developed by Richard FitzHugh and Jin-ichi Nagumo, but it captured the key behaviors of neurons, such as spiking, their refractory period, etc.

Mapping the Oscillatory Rhythm of the Brain

The cognitive function of the human brain can not be studied by the activity of individual neurons alone, since these functions emerge from the coordinated, rhythmic activity of large populations of neurons, organized into networks that span multiple brain regions. This coordinated activity gives rise to oscillatory rhythms, which are periodic fluctuations in neural activity. These rhythms are not mere byproducts of neural activity but are fundamental to the brain's ability to process information, integrate sensory inputs, and support higher-order cognition. We studied briefly about these oscillatory patterns of the brain in chapter 2, which are grouped into distinct bands (refer to the table), each associated with different cognitive and physiological states. Below is a quick recap before we move on to discuss a mathematical model.

Frequency Band	Range (Hz)	Main Activities	Primary Brain Regions
Delta	0.5–4	Deep sleep, healing, restorative processes	Thalamus, cortex (during sleep)
Theta	4–8	Attention, memory encoding, and sensory integration	Hippocampus, prefrontal cortex
Alpha	8–12	Relaxed wakefulness, inhibition of irrelevant sensory input	Occipital cortex, parietal areas
Beta	13–30	Sensorimotor activities, alertness, and maintaining active tasks	Sensorimotor cortex, frontal regions
Gamma	30–100	Attention, feature binding, complex sensory integration	Visual cortex, associative cortical areas

> ### *A quick recap of how oscillatory patterns emerge*
>
> The neuronal spike, modelled by the Hodgkin-Huxley equations, enables a neuron to transmit signals to other neurons via synaptic transmission. Neurons are either excitatory or inhibitory. Excitatory Neurons release neurotransmitters like glutamate, which depolarize postsynaptic neurons and promote further spiking. Inhibitory Neurons release GABA, which hyperpolarizes postsynaptic neurons and suppresses spiking. Together, they form a feedback loop where an excitatory neuron's spike activates other excitatory neurons and amplified activity, and in the process, inhibitory neurons also get activated, which then suppress excitatory neurons, creating a negative feedback loop that stabilizes the network. This interplay results in a rhythmic population activity, usually called as Oscillatory pattern of the brain.

The brain oscillations, observed in frequency bands such as delta (0.5–4 Hz), theta (4–8 Hz), alpha (8–12 Hz), beta (12–30 Hz), and gamma (30–100 Hz), act as a temporal scaffold that aligns spikes across neurons and brain regions. The synchronization of spikes within oscillatory cycles binds neural activity into meaningful patterns. Oscillations in different frequency bands interact through cross-frequency coupling, where the phase of a slower rhythm (such as theta) modulates the amplitude of a faster rhythm (such as gamma), which supports hierarchical organization of neural activity. In the hippocampus, gamma oscillations are nested within theta cycles, which enables the brain to encode multiple items within a single theta cycle. This is critical for working memory and episodic memory, as it allows the brain to maintain and manipulate multiple representations simultaneously. (John E Lisman 2013).

Imagine you are trying to remember a phone number someone just told you while walking through a busy market. As you repeat the digits in your head, your brain's theta oscillations (4–8 Hz) in the hippocampus create a temporal framework, which organizes the sequence of digits into a single chunk within a theta cycle. Nested gamma oscillations (30–100 Hz) encode each digit and bind them into a coherent memory. This theta-gamma coupling allows you to hold and manipulate the phone number in your working memory, despite the distracting noise and sights around you, until you can write it down.

Brain oscillations not only support integrated cognitive functions (such as sensory processing and memory retrieval) but also regulate the flow of information by enhancing relevant signals and suppressing noise. For example, when we are listening to a sound carefully, alpha activity (8–12 Hz) increases in the visual cortex of the brain to turn down visual input, so that we are less distracted by what we see. But these are brief moments of inhibition, like a gate that opens or closes at regular intervals, which helps the brain organize attention in time, so that it doesn't get overwhelmed by too much information at once.

When we are performing a complex task, such as solving a mathematical problem, multiple cognitive processes are engaged, including a network of brain regions such as the Prefrontal Cortex (working memory, attention), the Parietal Cortex (spatial reasoning) (Stanislas Dehaene 2003) and Hippocampus (retrieval and relational reasoning) (Eichenbaum 2001), act together to help us stay focused while solving the problem, and at the same time, recall and retrieve relevant concepts related to the problem and combine the retrieved data with the presented information to derive a solution.

The oscillatory rhythms generated by synchronized neural populations are detectable through EEG, which is a non-invasive technique that measures Local field potentials (LFPs), which are the electrical potentials recorded in the extracellular space of the brain, resulting from the summed activity of many neurons, particularly their synaptic and dendritic currents, primarily from the cortex region, and exhibit characteristic oscillatory patterns in the aforementioned frequency bands. Unlike action potentials, which are brief and localized spikes described by the Hodgkin-Huxley model, LFPs reflect the slower, more sustained currents associated with synaptic inputs and dendritic processing (Buzsáki 2012).

These patterns are analysed to study brain function in various contexts, from clinical diagnostics (such as detecting epileptic seizures) to cognitive neuroscience (such as investigating attention or memory). For example, during a working memory task, EEG recordings often show increased gamma power in the prefrontal cortex, which indicates heightened neural synchronization associated with maintaining and manipulating information. (Marc W Howard 2001).

To model LFPs and the oscillatory patterns they exhibit, a framework is needed that simulates the collective activity of neural populations and their contributions to extracellular fields. Single-neuron models like Hodgkin-Huxley lack the capacity to represent these population-level phenomena, as they do not account for the spatial organization of neurons or the temporal coordination required for LFP generation. Even if an attempt is made to map out the network through the Hodgkin-Huxley model, it will be a computationally expensive task, which will involve solving four differential equations for each neuron, and simulating thousands or millions of neurons with realistic synaptic connections. Thus, neural mass models and network models must be employed to simplify the description of neural populations. The Wilson-Cowan model is one such model, which we will be discussing.

The Wilson-Cowan Model

By the mid-20th century, neuroscience had established that neurons fire action potentials when stimulated above a threshold, and networks of such neurons with excitatory and inhibitory connections could perform complex computations (Pitts 1943). McCulloch and Pitts proposed a mathematical model in 1943, where neurons acted like logic gates, and any complex function could be built from these simple building blocks. However, a unified, tractable model was missing that would incorporate both excitatory and inhibitory populations explicitly and describe their collective dynamics over time. McCulloch and Pitts model was heavily criticized by Shimbel and Rapoport in their paper "*A statistical approach to the theory of the central nervous system*" (Rapoport 1948), who argued that the model was too rigid and unrealistic for biological systems and advocated for a more biologically plausible approach which focussed on brain's adaptive quality and dynamic behavior.

They created a mathematical model to predict how likely it is that neurons in a specific brain region will fire at the next time step based on the type and number of synapses (connections) a neuron has and the strength and threshold of the signal. This model did not focus on a single neuron but targeted a fraction of neurons in a certain region. No matter how elegant the theory seemed, the calculations were complex since the details of every synapse (its strength, location, type) would be needed, and these details are microscopic and complex in nature themselves. But it propelled a shift from trying to build precise logical circuits to trying to understand population behavior in a statistical and dynamic way.

During the 1970s, Hugh R. Wilson and Jack D. Cowan were working at the University of Chicago. Wilson, a physicist by training, and Cowan, a mathematician and physicist with interests in biological systems, were influenced by the growing field of theoretical neuroscience, which aimed to apply mathematical and physical principles to brain function.

We know already that the brain oscillations arise from the coordinated activity of many neurons, not just one. These oscillations are visible in EEG recordings, which measure electrical signals from the brain's surface, and they reflect local field potentials (LFPs), which are the combined electrical activity of many neurons.

Wilson and Cowan developed their model to describe the temporal evolution of two interacting neural populations: excitatory (E) and inhibitory (I). One can think of excitatory neurons as cheerleaders, encouraging other neurons to fire, and inhibitory neurons as referees, calming things down to prevent chaos. The model assumes that the activity of each population is represented by its mean firing rate, which is influenced by inputs from other neurons, its current activity, and external stimuli. Instead of tracking every single neuron, the model looks at the average activity level of each group, say how "loudly" the excitatory and inhibitory neurons are firing.

$E(t)$ = *Mean firing rate of the excitatory population at time t*

$I(t)$ = *Mean firing rate of the inhibitory population at time t*

The firing rate is a simplification of neural activity, which ignores detailed membrane potential dynamics like in the Hodgkin-Huxley model, but captures the collective output of the population. The Wilson-Cowan model assumes that the rate of change of activity follows a first-order differential equation.

$$\frac{dE}{dt} = -Decay\ Term + Activation\ term$$

$$\frac{dI}{dt} = -Decay\ Term + Activation\ term$$

The '*decay term*' represents the natural tendency of neural activity to decrease if no new inputs are received. This is biologically realistic because neurons have a limited energy supply, and their firing rate diminishes without sustained synaptic input or external stimulation. Since it is a linear process proportional to the current activity, it is represented by a *decay rate constant, α.* Biologically, it reflects the membrane time constant and synaptic decay, typically on the order of milliseconds to tens of milliseconds in cortical neurons. (Dayan 2001).

The '*activation term*' represents how inputs drive the population's firing rate. The total input to the excitatory population is represented by the following equation:

$$E_a = c_{EE}E - c_{IE}I + P_E$$

$$I_a = c_{EI}E - c_{II}I + P_I$$

Here, excitatory neurons that excite each other are represented by $c_{EE}E$ and inhibitory neurons that inhibit each other are represented by $c_{II}I$. The excitatory neurons that excite inhibitory neurons are represented by $c_{EI}E$ and inhibitory neurons that inhibit excitatory neurons are represented by $c_{IE}I$. The coefficients attached to E and I neurons represent excitatory and inhibitory synaptic strengths. The negative sign reflects the suppressive effect of inhibitory inputs and P_E, P_I are external inputs.

However, the above equations don't directly translate into firing rates because neurons have a nonlinear response. For example, a weak input may produce no firing, while a strong input causes rapid firing, but there's a maximum rate beyond which neurons can't fire faster. This nonlinearity is modelled using a *sigmoid activation function, S,* which mimics the firing rate response of neurons to synaptic input.

Since neurons have a refractory period after firing, during which they are less responsive to new inputs. To account for this, Wilson and Cowan included a scaling factor that acts upon the activation term and reduces the effective population size available to fire. The activation terms can be further elaborated as:

$$E_a = (k_E - rE) \cdot S_E(c_{EE}E - c_{IE}I + P_E)$$

$$I_a = (k_I - rI) \cdot S_I(c_{EI}E - c_{II}I + P_I)$$

Here, k_E and k_I represent maximum possible firing rates (or population sizes) for excitatory and inhibitory neurons. r is the refractory parameter that represents the fraction of neurons that are temporarily unresponsive due to recent firing. E and I are current firing rates that reduce the available population. By putting it all together, the original Wilson-Cowan equations take the following form:

There Is No A.I.

$$\frac{dE}{dt} = -\alpha E + (k_E - rE) \cdot S_E(c_{EE}E - c_{IE}I + P_E)$$

$$\frac{dI}{dt} = -\alpha I + (k_I - rI) \cdot S_I(c_{EI}E - c_{II}I + P_I)$$

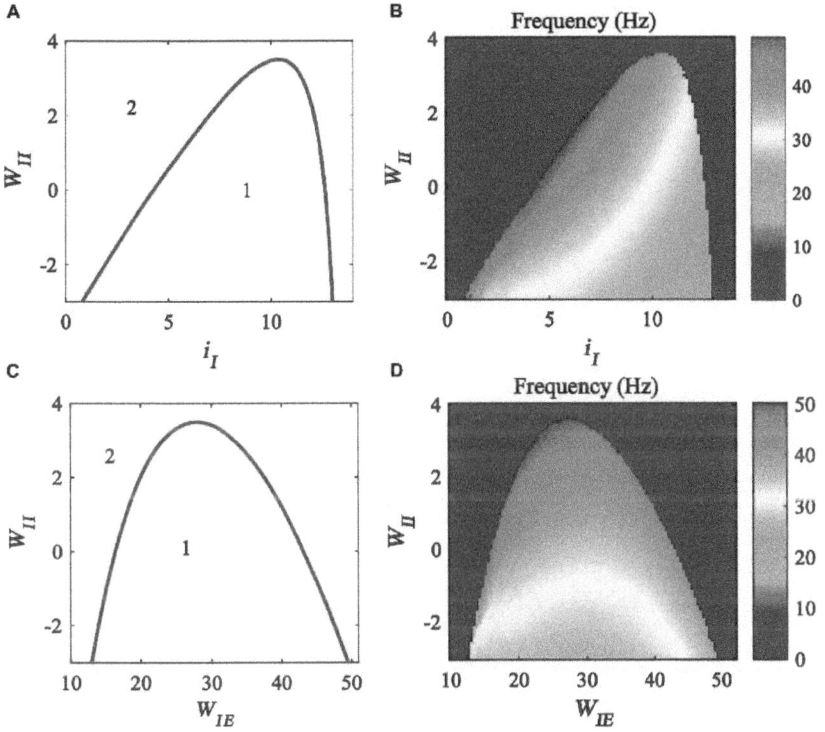

Figure 20 Influences of the interaction of inhibitory self-feedback and inhibitory input or coupling strength on the dynamic behavior of the Wilson-Cowan model. (A) The codimension two bifurcations with respect to iI and WII; (C) The codimension two bifurcations with respect to WIE and WII; (B,D) Oscillation frequency distribution diagrams. The area labelled 1 represents limit cycle oscillations, the area labelled 2 represents fixed-point states, and the blue curve represents Hopf bifurcation curves. Source: https://www.frontiersin.org/journals/systems-neuroscience/articles/10.3389/fnsys.2022.723237/full

The above equations are coupled, nonlinear differential equations because E and I depend on each other through the input terms (the feedback loop), and the sigmoid functions introduce nonlinearity. These equations describe how the firing rates evolve over time, driven by excitatory-inhibitory interactions and external inputs.

The Wilson-Cowan equations lead to oscillatory dynamics through the interplay of excitatory and inhibitory feedback. To analyse oscillations, we can linearize the equations around a fixed point (steady state) and compute the eigenvalues of the system's Jacobian matrix. If the eigenvalues have a positive real part and a non-zero imaginary part, the system exhibits damped or sustained oscillations. By numerically solving the equations (using Euler or Runge-Kutta methods), we can simulate $E(t)$ and $I(t)$ over time. The resulting time series often shows oscillatory patterns, with frequencies determined by the parameters.

End Note

Now that we have studied how neurons in the human brain are modelled, we can draw comparisons with the modelling of present-day A.I. models and see for ourselves whether they are actually *intelligent*.

Is A.I. really Intelligent?

It matters little who first arrived at an idea, rather what is significant is how far an idea can go. – Sophie Germain.

Before we start any discussion about LLM models being intelligent, it would be ideal to understand briefly what intelligence stands for.

Intelligence is a fundamental entity, and perception is merely a result. Intelligence is the art of decision making. Choosing from options is statistical. Intelligence is characterized by judgment, discrimination, knowledge, ascertainment, will, virtue, and detachment.

As per Sankhya Literature, Prakriti, the primordial material matrix of the physical universe, when churned by *'gunas'*, the first evolute emerging from it is Intelligence or 'buddhi'. These *'gunas'* are catalysts in the evolution of the material universe when there is interaction between *'Prakriti'* and *'Purusa'*. And it is due to specific intermixture and proportionality of *gunas*, living beings exhibit different mindsets and psychological dispositions.

The word "intelligence" has its roots in Latin and evolved through several languages before reaching modern English. The Latin word "intelligentia" means "understanding", "discernment", or "the faculty of perception". The Latin "intelligentia" passed into Old French as "intelligence," and only by the 14th century, intelligence entered English through Anglo-French and Middle English. But with time, its meaning expanded to include "information (e.g., "intelligence reports")" and "superior cognitive ability (e.g., reasoning, learning, problem-solving, etc.)".

So, what does this shift in the perspective of one single word tell us?

"What has been is what will be, and what has been done is what will be done; and there is nothing new under the sun". - The book of Ecclesiastes (chapter 1, verse 9, Revised Standard Version).

Nature is both periodic and perpetual. However, a moment never repeats itself. Here is a paradox to trouble your mind. There is an old Greek saying, which is attributed to Heracleitus of Ephesus, *"Upon those who step into the same rivers, different and ever different waters flow down"*.

We live in a complex world, and our trajectory in this multi-dimensional plane is non-linear. Our brain, which performs the cognitive tasks for us, helps us navigate through this plane by charting its unique trajectory based on the experiences gained over the years and genes passed down by our ancestors. It would be safe to say that every human being, if we choose not to consider all living beings, has their own trajectory and is unique in a sense. The question then arises, *"Can such a unique entity be compared and replaced by a generalized probabilistic model?"*.

And the answer to such a question can only be realized by understanding the limitations of human research about various aspects of brain functioning.

Intelligence is not computable

Sir Roger Penrose, the Nobel prize-winning scientist and philosopher, explores the idea that the word "Intelligence", at least in the standard usage, implies "understanding" and "understanding" requires some "awareness" or "consciousness". When the idea of a mechanical entity being intelligent is floated around, it silently implies that the entity has some consciousness, and generically, it boasts its ability to compute intelligence. When computation is invoked, numbers come into play. The idea is to represent the "intelligence" of an individual in terms of numbers. Let us introspect on this viewpoint.

For a moment, let us hypothetically entertain this wild idea that the individuality of a person has nothing to do with any individuality that one might try to assign to his material constituents. Say, it can be represented in terms of some configurations, and these configurations can then be represented in another form such as matrices of numbers, from which it can be recovered back again to the original form. The question arises whether the configurations represented in terms of numbers and encoded on a hard drive can be claimed to represent the individuality of a person? To be more concise, if we ignore physical configurations and explicitly focus on encoding the mental configurations of a person on the disk, then the disk that holds the configurations of an individual's intelligence can be recognized as the individual himself. Moreover, if another individual is now created out of the same configurations, can the new individual claim the same identity as the original one? Does this imply that at this point, the same consciousness is at two places at once (*say we chose to ignore the consciousness encoded in the magnetic disk*)? Moreover, if the original individual somehow dies in a fatal accident by the fate of luck, will the relatives of this original one accept the duplicated individual as the original one without any sense of loss? (Penrose 1989).

The scenarios above seem a little paradoxical, and one may even argue that they are completely hypothetical. Let us take another try, but this time in the mathematical realm.

Say, scientists have designed a very smart AI chatbot, which they claim to be "*intelligent*". It has been fed all the rules of arithmetic, logic, and some powerful theorems, and moreover, it has access to the most advanced computational resources, which make it lightning fast. One may ask this chatbot, "*Can it prove every mathematical truth?*". And at first glance, we may expect the answer to be "*Yes*", since it has been fed everything we had. It is now time to add a twist to the story.

We construct a special statement S inside the chatbot that says: "*This statement is not provable by Chatbot.*" There are two possible scenarios. If Chatbot proves S, then S is false since S says it cannot be proved. If the chatbot cannot prove S, then S is true as it claims. In essence, S is a true statement that this intelligent chatbot cannot prove.

In fact, this idea is not new. It is based on the incompleteness theorems published by Kurt Gödel in 1931. In his first theorem, Gödel suggested that no matter how carefully we design a consistent formal system capable of expressing arithmetic, there will always be true statements about numbers that the system cannot prove. In his second theorem, he suggested, any consistent formal system that is sufficiently expressive to describe basic arithmetic cannot prove its consistency. By formal systems, he meant a rigorous mathematical framework used to derive theorems, which are true statements, from a set of axioms (assumed truths) using strict rules of inference.

Invoking Gödel's theorems, Sir Roger Penrose argues that recognizing a truth requires insight that is beyond mechanical following of rules. One must go outside the formal system to recognize the truth. Historically, this has been done many times, but insights have often taken centuries to come. Take the case of the expansion of the number system. Initially, we had natural numbers, then we discovered integers, then rational numbers, and irrational numbers to fill the gaps in the number line. However, to understand the significance of a simple calculation $\sqrt{-1}$, a problem which haunted the mathematicians for centuries, the very insight to transcend the one-dimensional plane of numbers and look into the *lateral* plane, which we know as the *complex* plane, took many centuries.

It is for the same reasons, humans can understand truths that a mechanical system cannot, as these systems are defined by humans only. To fill the gaps in understanding, one must elevate oneself to the next level. This has always been the case. Eventually, persistence on the path of knowledge pays off, and mathematicians were rewarded with complex numbers (a combination of real numbers and imaginary units present in the lateral or complex plane), which opened the door to solving equations of multiple dimensions. More importantly, it opened the door to the Quantum world, which is the key to understanding the world in its purest form. Since the A.I. systems run on computable processes, they are fundamentally limited and cannot be claimed as *"intelligent"*. The idea that Sir Penrose is trying to paint is that *Computation* and *Determinism* are two different aspects. A system can be deterministic, but that does not mean it can be computed by algorithms. *Determinism* means that the system's future is entirely fixed by its current state and rules, with no randomness involved. And *Computability* means there exists an algorithm (a finite, mechanical procedure) that can compute or predict the system's future states.

And to prove this point, he invokes the findings of the very person who designed the computable machines in the first place, Alan Turing. He refers to the *halting problem* of a universal Turing machine which asks whether there exists a general algorithm (or Turing machine) that can determine, for any given Turing machine *(T)* and input *(x)*, whether *(T)* will halt (stop running after a finite number of steps) or run forever. And Turing himself proved by contradiction that no such general algorithm exists.

Suppose we have a Turing machine *(H)*, referred to as the *halt checker*, which takes two inputs: A description of a given Turing machine *(T)* and an input *(x)* for that Turing machine. When we run the halt checker, it outputs "Yes" if *(T)* halts on input *(x)* or else "No". We can then use our halt checker to create a new Turing machine, say *(D)*, but with a *twist!*

(D) takes a single input: the description of a Turing machine *(T)*. It runs the halt checker *(H)* on *(T)* with the description of a given Turing machine *(T)*. Functionally *(D)* does exactly the opposite of what the halt checker *(H)* outputs. If *(H)* says *(T)* stops when given its description, then *(D)* goes into an infinite loop. Or else, if *(H)* predicts that *(T)* does not halt, then *(D)* halts immediately. *Basically, (D) is the child who does exactly the opposite of what a teacher asks.* Let us give *(D)* a taste of its own medicine and run *(D)* on its own description. Here is the sequence that follows:

(D) feeds its description to the halt checker *(H)* and *(H)* predicts whether *(D)* halts when run on its own description. There are two possible outcomes from this process. According to *(D)*'s design, if *(H)* says *(D)* halts, then *(D)* is supposed to go into an infinite loop. But this contradicts *(H)*'s prediction, because *(H)* said *(D)* halts, yet *(D)* is now looping forever. In another possible scenario, if *(H)* says *(D)* does not halt, then it should halt immediately. Since the very assumption of the existence of such a halt checker *(H)* or *fortune teller* leads to a contradiction, the very assumption must be false.

The halting problem shows a fundamental limit to computation. Even though a Turing machine's behavior is deterministic, we cannot always predict its outcome using a general algorithm. In the same way, the universe's evolution can be deterministic, but its further states are not computable. And the very fact that the accuracy with which the initial data related to our universe can be known is always limited, abiding by the nature of differential equations, where a small deviation from the input can lead to an absolutely enormous change in the resulting behaviour, it is impossible to predict the chaotic nature of the universe. (Penrose 1989).

To explain the non-computational aspects of human intelligence, Sir Penrose turns to quantum mechanics because it introduces elements of non-determinism and non-local effects through entanglement, which may be crucial to understanding the holistic integration of information in the brain. In simple terms, it is the resonance of quantum equations with the complex plane that gives hope to Penrose's proposal. However, he instructs to proceed with caution, and this scepticism of quantum mechanics was well echoed by its foundational figures, Niels Bohr, Schrödinger, Einstein, and Paul Dirac. In the words of Paul Dirac, who set up the general framework of quantum mechanics, *"Quantum mechanics is a provisional theory. Why should I look for an answer in quantum mechanics?"* Einstein famously called quantum phenomena *"spooky action at a distance"* in his debate with Bohr, and Bohr himself cautioned, *"Those who are not shocked when they first come across quantum theory cannot possibly have understood it"*.

In Quantum mechanics, the state of an entity (a particle or system) is represented by a wave function. $\psi(x,t)$. It is a complex-valued function of position and time that encodes all possible information about the system, such as its position, momentum, and energy. It is the complex nature of ψ that allows us to represent both amplitude (magnitude) and phase (angle in the complex plane). The phase is related to the *imaginary* part, which finds its representation in the complex plane and helps to determine how different quantum states combine. For example, in the famous double-slit experiment, the probability of a particle's position depends on the interference of complex amplitudes, leading to patterns that real numbers cannot replicate.

Quantum systems exist in a superposition of states, which means they are described by a linear combination of wave functions.

$$\psi = c_1\psi_1 + c_2\psi_2 + ..$$

This does not mean that the system is present in one state or the other, but it is present in a state that is a combination of all possible states. Let us understand this through a simple analogy. Imagine Cristiano Ronaldo entering the football scene at a very young age, before he was recognized by the talent scouts of Manchester United. His career could have taken many possible paths from that point onwards. If he had not maintained his work ethic, he would have even retired by the age of 30, which most footballers do. Or maybe, he would have been recognized by another team of talent scouts and put under a manager who would not have nurtured his talents the way Alex Ferguson did. One can say, at the point in time, he was a combination of all possible states. However, the CR7, which we know today, exists only because of the sequence of decisions taken at a crucial juncture, or else there could have been multiple possibilities in which his career would have branched out. But hold on, this is just an analogy, and not a simplistic take on the Quantum theory.

The point being, a system can be present in a linear combination of multiple states, but the very moment we try to infer anything from the system, it results in a definite reality, which is called the *wave function collapse*. It is the process by which a quantum system, upon measurement, transitions from a superposition of multiple states to a single definite state. After this point, the system is no longer in superposition but in a definite state. The other possible states are effectively lost and no longer remain inaccessible. The system is described solely by the collapsed state, and from this point, the system evolves according to the time-dependent Schrödinger equation. The detailed explanation of this process is not in the scope of the current discussion. The reader is, however, encouraged to dive deeper into this topic as it may present some intriguing insights.

Penrose proposes that quantum superposition, where a system exists in multiple states simultaneously until measured, could enable non-computational processes in the brain, which he argues are necessary for consciousness and cannot be replicated by classical systems. In his famous yet controversial Orchestrated Objective Reduction (Orch-OR) Hypothesis, he proposes that consciousness emerges from quantum processes in microtubules, orchestrated by biological processes in the brain, with a specific mechanism called Objective Reduction (OR) driving the process. Microtubules are cylindrical protein structures made of tubulin dimers, forming part of the cytoskeleton in cells, including neurons. They provide structural support, facilitate intracellular transport, and play roles in cell division and signaling. In the Orch-OR hypothesis, tubulin dimers in microtubules are hypothesized to enter superpositions of different conformational states. For example, a tubulin dimer might be in a superposition of "up" and "down" configurations. These superpositions are maintained in a coherent state, meaning the quantum states preserve their phase relationships, potentially protected from environmental noise by biological mechanisms. Penrose proposed a novel mechanism for wavefunction collapse called Objective Reduction (OR), where a superposition collapses into a definite state when the gravitational self-energy, related to the spacetime curvature differences between superposed states, reaches a critical threshold. (Hameroff 2014).

The above hypothesis builds on some established science but extends into speculative territory. Traditionally, biological systems were thought to be too "warm and wet" for quantum coherence to survive due to rapid thermal decoherence. However, recent studies in photosynthetic complexes have shown that quantum coherence can assist energy transfer even at biological temperatures, suggesting that quantum effects in biology may be possible. Craddock et al. investigated the feasibility of quantum coherent energy transfer in microtubules, hypothesizing that the aromatic amino acids (notably tryptophan residues) in tubulin could support similar quantum coherent energy transfer. They employed molecular dynamics simulations and quantum mechanical calculations to model energy transfer between tryptophan residues in tubulin and accounted for the protein environment by using the experimentally measured optical dielectric constant of tubulin, which significantly affects coupling strengths between chromophores. The dielectric constant is a number that tells us how a material affects electric fields passing through it.

Contrary to earlier assumptions using low dielectric constants, their calculations showed non-negligible dipolar couplings (up to 60 cm^{-1}) between specific tryptophan pairs, which indicated the potential for coherent excitonic interactions. When excitons, which are packets of energy created when electrons in molecules are excited by energy (e.g., thermal or vibrational), interact coherently, they can transfer energy efficiently and quickly across molecules without losing much energy. The researchers further applied the Haken-Strobl model to simulate exciton population dynamics under thermal fluctuations, showing that coherent energy transfer could persist for short timescales (picoseconds to nanoseconds) despite environmental noise, though this is shorter than the timescales proposed by the Orch-OR hypothesis. (Travis John Adrian Craddock 2016). Although this study supports the biological feasibility of such quantum processes in microtubules and provides computational evidence that microtubules have the structural and energetic properties necessary to support quantum coherent energy transfer, the experimental validation of quantum coherence in microtubules at the cellular level is still lacking.

Moreover, the process of wave function collapse is neither deterministic nor random. The laws behind the collapse are not known to humans yet and are not computable for the same reason. This is what Erwin Schrödinger tried to explain through his famous cat thought experiment. Even Schrödinger himself did not believe the cat was literally dead and alive simultaneously. He presented this thought experiment to illustrate the incompleteness of Quantum theory in the traditional interpretation.

In Schrodinger's imaginary experiment, a cat is placed in a box with a tiny bit of radioactive substance. When the radioactive substance decays, it triggers a Geiger counter, which causes a poison or explosion to be released that kills the cat. Now, the decay of the radioactive substance is governed by the laws of quantum mechanics. This means that the atom starts in a combined state of *"going to decay"* and "not going to decay". If we apply the observer-driven idea to this case, there is no conscious observer present since everything is in a sealed box, so the whole system stays as a combination of the two possibilities. The cat ends up both dead and alive at the same time. Because the existence of a cat that is both dead and alive at the same time is absurd and does not happen in the real world, this means the wavefunction collapses are not just driven by conscious observers. Even Einstein saw the same problem with this dual state existing simultaneously. In fact, every interaction a quantum particle makes can collapse its state. To experience the superposition of the cat, the observer must himself be superimposed in multiple realities.

A quantum system can be described precisely using Schrodinger's equations, which when given the initial state of the system can help in calculating what the system will be doing in future at a certain point, however, when it comes to measurement, we do not get a single answer but the probabilities of certain outcomes. No wonder, the Quantum theory is regarded as *incomplete* by many scientists. Thus, it will be safe to accept the notion for now that the understanding of *intelligence* is not clear for the time being.

The Problem of Complex Connectivity and Function

The two mathematical models that we covered in our discussion in the last chapter present a very minuscule overview of the brain's neural connectivity. For example, the Hodgkin-Huxley model treats neurons as computational units that process inputs via synaptic potentials and produce outputs through action potentials. It tries to paint a classical and deterministic framework to present the brain's neuronal activity, and hence fails to present the complete picture of consciousness, as it fails to account for the non-computational aspect of the brain which involves the processes at smaller scales, such as molecular or quantum levels.

Even after extensive study of brain structure over the past few decades, the principles governing the complex interconnectivity of neurons and their relationship to function remain elusive. The brain's functionality depends on how neurons are interconnected and how these connections enable coordinated activity. This is not just a matter of wiring but of timing and synchronization across networks. The problem is that while we can observe these rhythms and their correlations with behavior, we lack a comprehensive theory of how connectivity patterns generate these dynamics or how specific oscillatory patterns map onto specific functions. Moreover, even the neural connections are not fixed; they change through synaptic plasticity, driven by experience and learning.

Buzsaki, in his work "Rhythms of the brain", discusses this elusive problem at greater length. He presents a peculiar insight about temporal scale preservation across brain sizes, to underline the fact that we still do not know as much about brain functions as we think. For example, the contraction speed of muscles, determined by the conserved properties of the protein myosin, is similar across mammals (such as humans, mice, and elephants). This implies that the neural mechanisms controlling these muscles must deliver signals within comparable time windows (10–100 ms) to achieve coordinated movement. Now consider the size of brains in mammals, which vary at greater length. Larger brains, such as those of elephants, have neurons spaced farther apart compared to smaller brains, like those of mice. This increased distance could, in principle, introduce delays in neural communication due to the relatively slow conduction velocity of neuronal axons. However, both small and large brains process information and generate responses within similar time frames to interact effectively with the world.

How does the brain ensure that functions like perception and action remain efficient and synchronized across different brain sizes, given the slow speed of neural conduction compared to, say, electronic circuits, where signals travel near the speed of light?

Memory and its mysteries

When a student is writing a paper in an exam, he takes some time to think about the data to be presented in the answer, but at the same time, once he formulates an answer, he picks up the pen and starts writing on the paper. He does not have to gather his thoughts about writing on paper, a skill mastered over the years.

Humans have generally two qualitative ways of storing information, one is declarative and the other is non-declarative. The declarative memory system is the system of memory that is perhaps the most familiar. It is the memory system that has a conscious component, and it includes the memories of facts and events. Examples of declarative memory are the ability to remember a phone number, the words to a song, or a past event. Nondeclarative memory (also referred to as procedural or implicit memory) is not available to consciousness, at least not in any detail, but is nevertheless extremely important. Such memories involve skills and associations that are generally acquired and retrieved at an unconscious level. Remembering how to shoot a basket or how to play the piano are examples of nondeclarative memories. It is, in fact, quite difficult to describe exactly how we do these things, and thinking about how to carry out automatic activities may disrupt the ability to perform them efficiently (al 2018).

However, even this broader level classification is debatable if we start considering genetic memories, which cover the aspect of the evolution of the brain wrought by millions of years of experience with behaviors that work and those that don't. A vast array of inherited behavior far outweighs what we learn in a single lifetime. But for the sake of our discussion, we can focus on the classification of the memory according to the time over which it is effective. There are three temporal classes of memory, which are generally acceptable, immediate memory, short-term memory (STM), and long-term memory (LTM).

Immediate memory is about holding on to the ongoing experience for a second or two, for example, our eyes blinking and taking a snapshot of the visible environment. If there is nothing of importance or to be alerted about, this memory is usually discarded.

The second category, the short-term memory (STM), also called working memory, is the ability to hold and manipulate information in the mind for seconds to minutes while it is being used to achieve a particular goal. While we are solving a mathematical problem, we are engaging our working memory by holding and manipulating numbers. Although STM is typically studied in the context of declarative memory, it also operates in the acquisition of nondeclarative information.

The last category, the Long-term memory (LTM), is about the ability to store information for an extended period, and it can range from days to a lifetime. Usually, information of some significance is transitioned from

STM to LTM. Skills by practice can also be embedded in long-term memory, such as once we learn how to drive a car, this skill serves throughout our lifetime.

In the context of memory, it must be noted that our ability to hold on to memories is directly correlated to or proportional to their significance in our lives. The normal human capacity for remembering relatively meaningless information is surprisingly limited (as noted, a string of seven to nine numbers or other arbitrary items), but can be enhanced by practice.

The ability to hold on to a piece of information temporarily to complete a task is specifically human. It causes certain regions of the brain to become very active, in particular the prefrontal lobe. This region, at the very front of the brain, is highly developed in humans. It is the reason that we have such high, upright foreheads, compared with the receding foreheads of our cousins, the apes. Clinical studies over the years have established the fact that the cerebral cortex is the major long-term repository for many aspects of declarative memory. Studies of amnesic patients have shown that the formation of declarative memories depends on the integrity of the hippocampus and its subcortical connections to the mammillary bodies and dorsal thalamus. All the pieces of information decoded in the various sensory areas of the cortex converge in the hippocampus, which then sends them back where they came from. The hippocampus acts

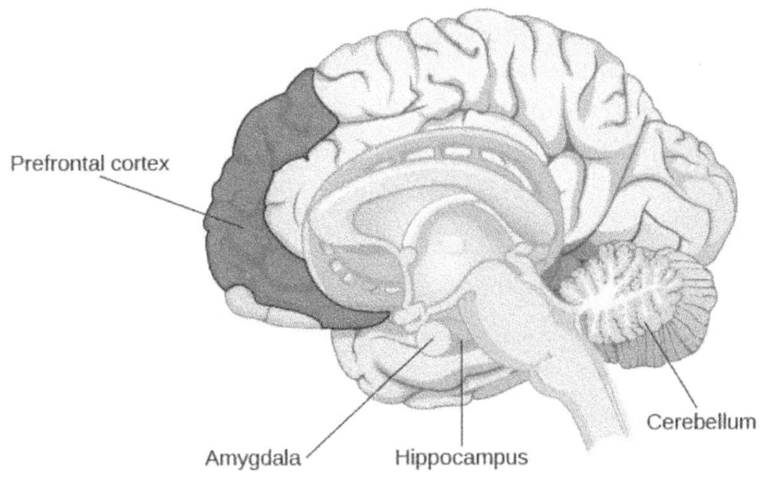

Figure 21 Brain areas that support declarative memory, source: https://opentextbc.ca/, licensed under CC BY-SA 4.0.

like a sorting centre where these new sensations are compared with previously recorded ones.

When we remember new facts by repeating them or by employing various mnemonic devices, we are passing them through the hippocampus several times. The hippocampus keeps strengthening the associations among these new elements until, after a while, it no longer needs to do so. The cortex will have learned to associate these various properties itself to reconstruct what we call a memory. (The Brain from Top to Bottom n.d.).

The hippocampus exhibits significant neural plasticity, which helps it to modify its neural circuits in response to experience, and thus it also creates associations among an object's various properties. This process is called Long-Term Potentiation (LTP), where synaptic strength between two neurons increases following their simultaneous activation (*remember? Neurons that fire together, wire together!).* LTP was discovered by Bliss & Lømo in 1973, which confirmed the theory of Donald Hebb, proposed way back in 1949.

However, the hippocampus cannot be considered the memory center of the brain. The reason is that long-term memory is not located in just one specific area of the brain. The hippocampus is the catalyst for long-term memory, but the actual memory traces are encoded at various places in the cortex. LTP is not exclusive to the hippocampus, and it has been observed in various cortical regions. These various cortical regions activated during an event would become so strongly linked with one another that they would no longer need the hippocampus to act as their link. This is called Systems Memory Consolidation. *Perhaps that is why music is so strongly related to nostalgia!*

The engram: The physical trace of memory

In 1923, German biologist Richard Semon proposed the engram theory of memory. According to this theory, when a person experiences something, a set of selected stimuli from this experience activates entire populations of neurons in that person's brain, thus inducing lasting chemical and physical changes in their connections. These changes are known as the *engram.* Each of the assemblies of neurons thus selected thereby contributes to the storage of the memory.

However, his theory received very little attention for decades until, in 1978, a group of researchers (Daniel L. Schacter, James Eric Eich, and Endel Tulving) reintroduced this theory into scientific discussions through their article *Richard Semon's theory of memory*. They aimed to re-evaluate Semon's work in light of modern cognitive psychology and neuroscience. They emphasized that Semon's theory anticipated numerous aspects of modern memory research, especially pattern completion being one of them. Pattern completion is the ability of the brain to reconstruct a complete memory from partial or degraded input. If part of the original sensory or contextual information is encountered again (*like a note of music*), this partial cue can activate the full neuronal assembly (engram) that represents the entire memory (*walk with your sweetheart*). They suspected that these assemblies of selected neurons may be the *engram*.

When Bliss and Lømo discovered LTP in 1973, they began to compile a lot of data about the cellular mechanisms of synaptic plasticity, such as the role of NMDA receptors, AMPA receptor insertion, calcium signalling, protein synthesis, and dendritic spine growth in LTP. (T V Bliss 1993).

Although these findings elucidated how individual synapses adapt to experience, but could not explain how these local changes scaled up to create a distributed engram capable of encoding complex memories and driving behavior. A breakthrough came with the development of optogenetics (2005), when Susumu Tonegawa and his team used this technology to identify and manipulate engram cells in mice. By artificially activating specific neurons that were active during learning, they could trigger memory recall. This was the first clear demonstration that reactivating a specific population of neurons could elicit memory recall.

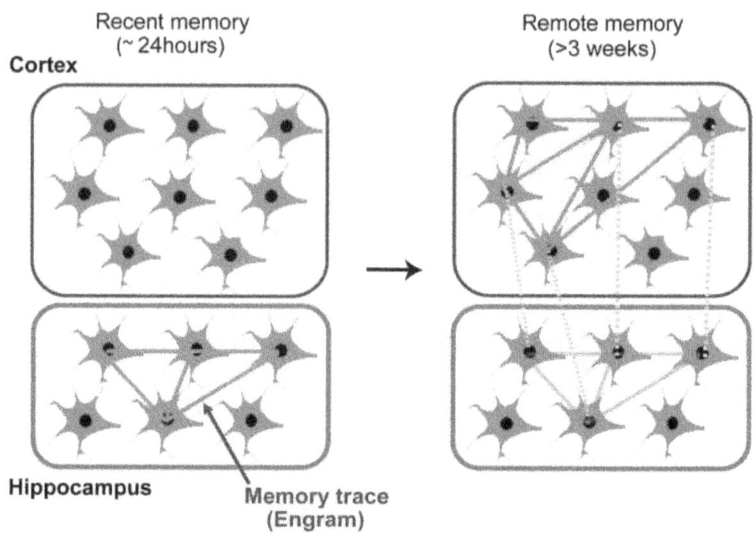

Figure 22 Systems Memory Consolidation

Its simpler interpretation means our synapses are never the same from one day to the next, because we are using them constantly, and so our memories are necessarily always in the process of being built and rebuilt.

However, the complete picture of the memory engram is still not clear. While LTP is a well-established model for synaptic strengthening, the specific molecular changes that distinguish engram synapses from non-engram synapses are unclear. For example, which proteins, receptors, or signaling pathways are uniquely involved in engram formation? Eric Kandel et al., in the book Principles of Neural Science (2021), note that while CREB-mediated gene expression and protein synthesis are critical for long-term memory, the full molecular cascade remains incomplete. It is also unclear how engram synapses encode the content and context of complex memories, such as episodic memories that integrate sensory, spatial, and emotional components. Episodic memories involve multiple dimensions (such as what, where, when, and emotional bonding), yet how these are represented in a distributed engram across the hippocampus, cortex, and amygdala is unknown. The role of subcortical structures, like the amygdala for emotional memories or the basal ganglia for procedural memories, in engram networks adds to the complexity. More importantly, how memory is chosen is not clear. How does the brain ensure that engram cells encode one memory and not others occurring simultaneously?

Forming a memory (neural connections of engram) is one thing, but how it is maintained is another aspect. Engrams must be stable to preserve memories over the years, but plastic enough to allow updating or integration with new information. The balance between stability and plasticity is a major unsolved question. For example, do engram synapses undergo continuous remodelling, or are they fixed after consolidation? (Josselyn n.d.).

But it is not just the neural circuits and their synchronization that pose the unanswered questions. There are other aspects, even at the broader level, that are not yet completely understood by the neuroscientists. For example, the split-brain research suggests that the two hemispheres of the brain have distinct functional specialization. The left hemisphere is dominant for language, logical reasoning, and analytical tasks, whereas the right hemisphere excels in visuospatial tasks, facial recognition, and holistic processing. However, the scope of split-brain research is quite limited due to the low number of split-brain patients, and hence these findings cannot be attributed to general behavior in the broader sense.

Nothing concrete about such mysteries of the brain has been formulated so far, and as it stands, science still has a lot of ground to cover to present a unified model of the brain.

What about the intelligence of A.I. model

The intelligence of a human is rooted in the brain, and the very fact that a unified model of the brain is far from complete, completely tosses out the claim of 'intelligence' in any model created by humans only. However, we shall be looking into the limitations of A.I. models to point out the data that verifies the previous statement.

Lack of Embodied Cognition

Consider having an A.I. model that can predict the probability of a picture being liked by a group of humans. Experimental data shows good convergence. However, real-life scenarios present more challenging dynamics that are hard to capture. For instance, researchers have conducted experiments in the past about smell affecting the cognitive ability of humans. They made a group of people sit in a room with a bad odour. They were then asked to review the pictures presented to them. These pictures have been curated based on their previous likes or dislikes. Surprisingly, members of that group did not approve some of the pictures, which they would have liked in an altogether different scenario. Now imagine planning an entire campaign based on the prediction of an A.I. model, yet losing out due to a small yet effective trigger. (Matheus Henrique Ferreira 2022).

A.I. models, aka Large Language Models (LLMs), lack embodiment and real-time interaction with a physical environment. They process text in a stateless, feedforward manner, with no intrinsic mechanism for synchronizing outputs to external temporal scales. For example, an LLM generating a response does not adjust its processing to match the timing of a real-world event. We have learnt in the first chapter of our discussion that LLMs rely on static, pre-trained weights in artificial neural networks. While these weights encode patterns from training data, they do not adapt in real-time to new contexts or physical constraints. Intelligence in biological systems involves coordinating perception, action, and cognition in real-time. It is very hard to replicate.

One may counter-argue that the weight of these A.I. models can be fine-tuned or specifically tuned to suit our needs. However, this argument does not take into account that fine-tuning a model is a computationally expensive task, and it is not even done periodically. To underline the computational ability of a human brain with respect to an A.I. model, let us look at the data.

Evaluating Cost of Operation

The brain operates primarily in 'survival' mode. It is an extraordinarily energy-efficient system that consumes approximately 20 watts of power to perform complex cognitive tasks, including perception, reasoning, memory, and motor control. This efficiency is maintained even though the brain employs a highly distributed, parallel architecture with approximately 86 billion neurons and 100 trillion synapses, which processes information concurrently across multiple regions. The brain focuses on conservation of energy by default, neurons fire sparsely at any given time for a specific task, and each spike consumes only a small amount of energy (on the order of 10^{-11} joules per spike) (Lennie 2003). This selective firing ensures that only relevant neural circuits are engaged. For example, in the visual cortex, only neurons tuned to specific features (e.g., edges, orientations) fire in response to a visual stimulus (D H HUBEL 1962).

Sparse processing of the brain is complemented by its ability to process the information, which is quite evident in tasks like pattern recognition. When recognizing a face, the brain processes features like shape, color, and motion in parallel across the fusiform face area, visual cortex, and other regions. These regions communicate via sparse synaptic connections. Now, out of the 20 watts (joules per second) for all cognitive functions, the brain spends only $\sim 10^{-5}$ to 10^{-3} joules per recognition event. (Attwell 2001).

Now, we can compare this cost in contrast to large language models for a similar task of pattern recognition. LLMs use dense matrix operations, across millions to billions of parameters, to perform pattern recognition by processing input data through layered architectures to identify linguistic or visual patterns. This processing involves tokenizing inputs (such as text or image embeddings), applying attention mechanisms, and computing activations across all layers. For text, this might mean identifying syntactic or semantic patterns, and for images, it involves feature extraction via vision transformers. Now, running a single inference on an LLM like GPT consumes significant energy, which depends on hardware and model size. A single forward pass for a 175-billion-parameter model on a GPU (e.g., NVIDIA A100) requires ~10^{12}–10^{13} floating-point operations (FLOPs). Assuming 0.4 picojoules per FLOP (typical for GPUs), this translates to ~0.4–4 joules per inference. For complex tasks like pattern recognition, inference may require multiple passes, which eventually raises costs to ~1–10 joules per event (Patterson 2021).

Okay, let us get to the training part, which is far costlier. Training a transformer model emits ~626,000 pounds of CO2, which is equivalent to ~300,000 kWh (1.08 x 10^{12}joules) (Strubell 2019).

The point is that the brain has evolved over millions of years to optimize energy use. While LLMs, designed for generality, still prioritize performance over efficiency, using brute-force computation. And even after consuming this much energy, they fail to learn incrementally in real time, which tells a lot about their intelligence. Nonetheless, there are numerous research initiatives in progress that are focused on the design of better hardware, with players like IBM and Intel dedicating a good number of resources to design affordable yet efficient chips.

Capturing non-linearity

A.I. models are not sentient beings but "stochastic parrots". Their capability is fundamentally statistical, driven by pattern matching rather than cognitive processes. LLMs learn to associate inputs with outputs based on probabilities derived from training data, without any inherent understanding of the underlying concepts or causal relationships. For example, when an LLM generates a response to a question, it does so by calculating the likelihood of certain words or phrases given the input context and completely relies on patterns observed during training. Unlike their counterparts, the mortal sentient beings, who can reason abstractly or infer causality, LLMs lack an internal model of the world that would allow them to understand why certain patterns exist or how they relate to real-world phenomena (Bender 2021).

We had discussed earlier in the first chapter about how LLMs capture non-linearity in data by using activation functions like ReLU or sigmoid, which allows them to approximate highly complex functions. This helps the models to capture intricate linguistic patterns, such as grammar, syntax, and even contextual nuances, to produce human-like text. However, this approximation is agnostic to meaning or intent. For instance, an LLM might correctly answer a factual question (such as, "What is the capital of France?") because it has seen similar patterns in its training data, not because it has any idea about the concept of a capital city of a country. Causal inference requires understanding why events occur, not just observing that they co-occur. LLMs might correctly predict that "smoking is linked to lung cancer" based on training data, but they cannot reason about the causal mechanisms (e.g., biological processes) unless explicitly trained on such explanations.

Similarly, when LLMs generate creative or persuasive text, they are not expressing intention but rather recombining patterns in ways that align with the input prompt. And quite evidently, they often struggle with tasks requiring them to go beyond their training scope, such as solving novel problems outside their training distribution or handling counterfactual reasoning. For instance, LLMs are not able to correctly answer queries about answer mathematical summation on an Excel sheet and therefore resort to measures like the use of an agent (tool), which is, in essence, *"automation"* rather than intelligence (Shanahan 2024). And even if we consider automation as a big breakthrough, one must stick to the ground reality while evaluating its projection in the future. Kamer Daron Acemoğlu, an economics professor at MIT, suggests in his paper, *"The Simple Macroeconomics of AI"*, that only 5% tasks are going to be automated in next 10 years and their contribution to the total factor productivity will be less than 1%, and its contribution to GDP will be no more than 1-2% if exaggerated (Acemoglu 2024). This comes as a sharp contrast in the light of claims made by McKinsey and Goldman Sachs, which suggest significant gains up to 7% in the GDP. The basis of his claims lies in the simple fact that so far, no critical applications have been developed for production processes by incorporating A.I. models. And this makes sense. A.I. models work well for predictable tasks that do not require social interaction and a high level of judgment. The current A.I. models perform well on easy to learn tasks, which have clear outcomes and are repetitive in nature, such as text summarization or image classification. However, on hard to learn tasks that require specific context, such as diagnosing complex conditions, strategic decision-making, etc., human judgment is relied upon. In general, most occupations require tacit knowledge that A.I. models or LLMs cannot reproduce. And because LLMs rely on pattern matching, they are prone to errors in out-of-distribution scenarios or when faced with adversarial inputs. For example, they may produce "hallucinations" (false but plausible outputs) when prompted with ambiguous or novel queries. Most tasks that we perform in real life do not just require recounting previous knowledge but demand improvisation.

There is often a discussion about why LLM writing feels bland, like a plethora of words vomited by the model without any emotion behind them. Steve Pinker, a cognitive psychologist and psycholinguist, discusses the reasons behind this in one of his interviews. He quotes Hamlet's famous quote, *"Brevity is the soul of wit"*, to explain his answer. The point is that LLMs are trained to output a generic response, which has been shaped to adhere to certain formats during their fine-tuning process over billions of examples. On the contrary, the classical literature seems beautiful, or poetic is because the authors were often constrained from multiple dimensions to present their thoughts on paper. More importantly, writing was the only medium of conveying the ideas to a wider audience back in the day. This motivated the writers to place themselves in the shoes of the audience and think accordingly. This required some serious mental effort. And on top of it, there were constraints from publishers about fitting the text within a certain length, which inspired the authors to think about presenting the text in a clearer yet concise manner. These kinds of mental exercises often resulted in texts that were not just beautiful but fresh. Writers were often challenged to think out of the box. Alas! Our A.I. writing assistants had the same intentions. But what are their intentions in reality? We will discuss next.

Intention of A.I.

Whom would you trust to fight the war of survival? Mercenaries who do not have a side to choose or anything to lose, or you will fall back to the loyal battalion of your army, who would give their lives to protect their motherland. We can make the question even simpler. If your wife is pregnant and in her last trimester, will you trust an autonomous driving car to navigate through traffic to reach the hospital, or will you show up for the task yourself?

If you count on safety and do not think of danger, if you do not know enough to be wary when enemies arrive, this is called a sparrow nesting on a tent, a fish swimming in a cauldron--they won't last the day. - Chuko Liang (A.D. 181-234)

Mercenaries are professional soldiers hired to fight for a foreign cause, who are typically motivated by financial gain rather than ideological or emotional ties. They can be deployed quickly without the bureaucratic constraints of national armies. One may even put forward an argument that, due to a lack of emotional investment in the conflict, they are more suited for objective decision-making. However, one must take note that they have no intrinsic allegiance to the cause.

During the 14th and 15th centuries, the fragmented Italian city-states such as Milan, Florence, and Venice often employed *condottieri* to wage war on their behalf. While these mercenaries brought military expertise, their loyalty was always contingent upon favourable terms. Such an entity is not united, ambitious, and without discipline, who fight to serve its purpose. Since mercenaries were paid per campaign rather than for victory, they had a financial incentive to avoid swift resolution. Some even negotiated with opposing forces to stage theatrical battles that minimized casualties while preserving the illusion of conflict. For instance, the *condottiere* Francesco Sforza, who at different points served Milan, Naples, and the Papal States, was notorious for manipulating his alliances to secure greater power and wealth. Eventually, he took control of Milan itself, proclaimed himself the duke (Machiavelli 1908).

Human cognition is deeply shaped by evolutionary pressures, where survival and reproduction have prioritized efficient, adaptive behaviors. When humans act in "survival mode" (under stress, scarcity, or threat), their decision-making often shifts toward rapid, heuristic-based solutions that conserve energy and maximize outcomes with minimal risk. For example, when faced with a predator, a human doesn't calculate probabilities but instinctively flees or fights. This efficiency is evolutionarily advantageous, as it conserves cognitive resources and prioritizes immediate survival. Humans build mental models of the world based on sensory experiences, social interactions, and causal relationships. This allows them to reason about "why" things happen and adapt to novel situations. A person might infer that a broken tool can be fixed with an alternative material based on an understanding of its function, even if they have never encountered that exact scenario. (Gigerenzer 2008).

LLMs, by contrast, are artificial systems with no survival instincts, personal stakes, or intrinsic motivation. They have "nothing to lose" because they lack agency, goals, or awareness of real-world consequences. Their objective is to maximize the likelihood of generating a coherent response, not to optimize for practical efficiency or survival. For example, when asked to solve a problem, an LLM might produce a verbose or overly general response because it is trained to cover probable outputs, not to minimize cognitive or temporal costs. When solving a problem, they draw on patterns seen in training data, not on an understanding of why those patterns exist. For instance, if asked how to fix a leaking pipe, an LLM might describe a common method (such as using tape) because it is frequently mentioned in texts, but it cannot reason about the pipe's material or the leak's cause unless explicitly prompted. Their inability to filter out irrelevant details or adapt to novel contexts can lead to less efficient solutions or, at times in choices which may incur the worst possible case.

While an A.I. model struggles with out-of-distribution tasks, Humans excel at generalizing to new contexts because they reason causally and draw on embodied experiences. *If one of your kin has to undergo a critical surgery, whom would you prefer? A trained surgeon who has a reputation for improvising under pressure and has tremendous experience, or an A.I. based machine who may have demonstrated more precision in surgical tasks but is not to be held responsible if things go the other way.*

Now, this discussion is not implying that humans always produce efficient solutions in survival-driven or practical contexts, and at times, A.I. models excel in specific scenarios, especially when the task is data-intensive or requires consistent output. But this makes them fall under the category of tools, which are used for a specific purpose, while the onus of performing the task end-to-end lies with the human in command.

And the irony of all this evolution of A.I. models is that even the makers of one model suite do not trust the intention of the other. Elon Musk, the Tesla CEO, has publicly raised questions about the intentions of contemporary tech companies, including Microsoft, OpenAI, and Google, while claiming Grok is the model one can trust. Yoshua Bengio, often regarded as the godfather of modern A.I., has publicly expressed concerns about the current state of A.I. development, terming it unsafe to use. His fear has been backed by different incidents across the world, where A.I. has been leveraged to obtain information about executing planned attacks and even deceiving systems. Bengio plans to develop *"a new AI model specifically designed to be safer than other AI models"*. Yuval Noah Harari, the celebrated historian, takes note of this wild race and distrust. He says in an interview that all the top tech CEOs pursuing A.I. race are in the race because they do not trust the technology in the hands of others. He raises concerns in his book, *Nexus: A Brief History of Information,* that *"The rise of machine-learning algorithms, however, may be exactly what the Stalins of the world have been waiting for. AI could tilt the technological balance of power in favor of totalitarianism"*. He specifically warns about the attempt to concentrate all information and power in one place, which may serve as a decisive advantage in the age of A.I. However, too much information for a model may also turn out to be its Achilles' heel, which we inspect next.

Model Collapse

Year 2024 saw frequent A.I. model releases from tech giants like Google, Amazon, Meta, OpenAI, etc. Newer Models were not just limited to generating text but could also generate pictures and videos based on user prompts. Results were no doubt fascinating. The Internet was all in praise for the new revolution in content creation. And when the dust of the storm settled, a good number of end users started to realize *all that glitters is not gold!*

Have you ever tried chatting with a GPT interface for longer contexts and only to realize it is talking in loops, as if an entity that promised to be so knowledgeable in the beginning, is now showing the signs of sudden aging? Answers coming out seemed to be just a repetition of previous ones, with some subtle twisting of words. Seems like you were not alone, it's just your frustration with the sudden dumbness of these large models did not find enough voice on social media, which is already manipulated by the bigger forces. Or maybe you just did not complain to anyone but tried to find faults in your prompting. After all, everyone else on the Internet seemed to be singing praise of the very same entity, which you found frustrating to convey your message or make sense to. Welcome to the new age virtual world, where everything is connected, yet one feels so much disconnected. But you can find solace now in 2025 that finally, some braver voices have found an audience, and this deliberately hidden dumbness of these models is being exposed and discussed. To find more comfort, draw the analogy to the Law of Diminishing Returns, which states that *as more of a variable input is added to a fixed input, the additional output produced eventually decreases after a certain point.*

This pattern is not limited to just text-generating models but is also evident in image or video-generating models. In mid-2024, users began noticing a decline in the output quality of MidJourney, a leading AI art generation platform that uses diffusion models to create high-quality, visually striking images from text prompts, particularly for prompts requiring creative or niche artistic styles. The issue became prominent around September–October 2024, when artists on X (formerly Twitter) and forums like Reddit reported that MidJourney's images were becoming repetitive, overly stylized, and prone to artifacts. Prompts like *"fantasy landscape"* or *"cyberpunk city"* produced near-identical images, often featuring cliched elements like castles on mountains or neon-lit skyscrapers with predictable layouts.

As per end users, earlier versions of MidJourney had offered more varied interpretations, such as unique architectural styles or unexpected color palettes. Niche prompts, like *"Gothic cathedral in a steampunk forest"* or *"minimalist Japanese ink painting,"* resulted in outputs that lacked specificity, defaulting to MidJourney's signature glossy, hyper-realistic aesthetic. This was a stark contrast to its earlier ability to capture diverse artistic styles. Some images showed visual glitches, such as distorted faces, unnatural lighting, or incoherent backgrounds (for example, trees merging into skies). These artifacts were particularly evident in complex or abstract prompts, where the model struggled to maintain coherence.

The issue gained traction when artists shared side-by-side comparisons on social media platforms, showing how MidJourney v6 (released in 2024) produced less detailed and diverse images than v5 for identical prompts. For example, a user posted a comparison for the prompt *"surreal desert oasis,"* noting that v5 generated varied scenes (e.g., crystalline pools, alien flora), while v6 repeatedly produced similar palm-tree-and-sand compositions with blurry edges.

The Shumailov et al study (Ilia Shumailov 2024) explained the above phenomenon as 'model collapse', where a generative model, trained iteratively on data that includes its outputs or those of similar models, progressively loses the ability to produce diverse, accurate, or high-quality outputs. Instead, the model's outputs converge toward a narrow, often degenerate distribution, amplifying biases, errors, or artifacts present in the synthetic data.

The devil lies in the details. LLMs are typically trained on large datasets scraped from the internet, books, or other text sources. Diffusion models like MidJourney rely on learning a probability distribution over images, guided by text prompts. As AI-generated content (from blog posts, code, and social media posts) proliferates, these datasets increasingly include synthetic data. Synthetic data often contains biases or errors introduced by earlier models (e.g., factual inaccuracies, cultural stereotypes). When models are retrained or fine-tuned on this mixed data, they ingest their outputs (or those of similar models) and end up creating a feedback loop. This recursion amplifies patterns in the synthetic data, such as stylistic quirks, biases, or errors, while diluting the diversity of the original human-generated data. Small errors in early synthetic data can lead to large-scale distortions in later iterations. Over time, the model's outputs become less representative of the true data distribution. For example, an LLM trained on AI-generated articles might overemphasize common phrases or topics (such as "AI is transformative") (Coldewey 2024). Imagine having a medical research paper generated by a very powerful large language model, say the DeepMind project of Google. Suppose it can guarantee you up to 95% accuracy, but what accounts for the 5% error present in the paper? Certainly, there needs to be a lot of discussion about the usage of the word 'intelligence' associated with Machine Learning, but the question is, are these voices actually going to reach us?

The Bigger Picture

But this reduction in diversity of voices being heard by an audience is not something newly associated with the content propelled by tech giants. On the record, in 2018, Facebook (now Meta) admitted its role in giving flares to social unrest in Myanmar. (Warofka 2018). One must not be naïve enough to consider it as an independent assessment of the faults of the algorithm, but it came on the backdrop of many public hearings and countless news reports pointing towards the role of biased algorithms. (Zaleznik n.d.).

Nothing in this world comes for free, and every process comes at a cost. Larry page, former Google CEO, once confessed to Kevin Kelly, the founding editor of Wired magazine, that Google is putting the search engine usage for free for a reason. And that reason was to acquire tons of data to create an A.I. and AI can turn lots of data into lots of power (Harari n.d.) . A drug dealer often starts giving freebees to young kids around the street corner, until they come back craving for more and ready to pay even with their lives. Ease of use is often a disguised attempt to take you farther from the truth. Here, one should not just limit the context of the word *'use'* with a commodity, but also extend it towards contemplation of idea. Humans long for validation and often prefer to get along with like-minded folks. But we have already learnt that our lives are not linear in nature. Hence, a wise man commits himself to add multiple dimensions (or perspectives) in the thought process for better decision making. Same goes for artistic abilities. More an artist has experienced life in its rarest form, better the output of his imagination with vivid details. Multi-perspective modelling reduces interpretive error. This requires time and effort to process the experience.

When a commodity is up for sale in mass, the business does not have time for patience. It runs on its own demands and supplies. And at times, demands have to be cooked. On social media, this is done by creating an echo chamber, where a user gets an ego boost (dopamine kick) quite frequently and returns for more. Social media platforms use machine learning models to predict user preferences based on past interactions (e.g., clicks, likes). These models prioritize content that align with a user's history and amplifies popular posts or those from like-minded communities. The user is less likely to stumble upon opposing views (Pariser 2011). However, in a most unlikely scenario, this pattern of *'ease'* has crept as a bug in A.I. models, and a lot of effort is being spent to cover it.

Current trend with A.I. models is to beat the performance benchmarks, much like social media platforms chased engagement metrics. But Charles Goodhart pointed to this obvious behavior way back in 1975, when he mentioned in his UK monetary policies that *"Measurement without purpose leads to manipulation, not progress"*. AI models are optimized for tasks that are easy to measure, and it leads to overfitting or gaming the system. Tech Companies train models specifically to excel on benchmark datasets, often at the expense of generalizability. A 2024 study found that some LLMs achieved near-perfect MMLU (Massive Multitask Language Understanding) scores but performed poorly on real-world tasks outside the benchmark's scope (Liao n.d.). Companies manipulate benchmarks by fine-tuning models on test data or exploiting dataset leaks (Greene 2025). The end result is supposed to be faulty. As Shrimad Bhagvad Gita prophesizes, *it is only through the non-attachment to outcomes, the right actions can be enabled.*

Remember, whether it is social media or A.I. models, they all remain valuable to their masters, if they can keep the end users engaged enough and craving for more. An illusion of *'ease'* is created, and creativity dies a silent death. The lure to get work done quickly and in turn quicker rewards, have historically created problems for the masses. We explore this idea more in the next chapter.

End Note

Now that we have discussed at length about the capabilities and limitations of A.I. models, we must now understand and analyse this sudden outpouring of love and push for the adoption of A.I. across every domain by big tech giants. As things stand in 2025, if any product is not backed by A.I., it lacks the killer instinct. But really?

<u>But A.I. revolution?</u>

Advertising has us chasing cars and clothes, working jobs we hate, so we can buy shit we don't need. - Tyler Durden, The Fight Club.

This is the year 2025, and the media has already claimed that it is an era of AI revolution. But revolution does not come one at a time. To be very specific, a revolution is about seeing a problem in a completely new light and recognizing some other problems for the first time. In the 1950s, when John von Neumann designed his first machines at the Institute for Advanced Study in Princeton, New Jersey, he started a revolution, but at the same time, he was also fascinated by weather forecasting. He believed wholeheartedly that weather modelling is an ideal task for a computer. Revolution brings with it days of unreal optimism, and rationality is hard to adhere to. Even a brilliant mind like Neumann ignored the simple fact that measurements are never perfect. And in a dynamic system, even a small change can lead to drastically different output. He overlooked the possibility of chaos with instability at every point. (Gleick 1988). All kinds of simulations were modelled on the computers and then on supercomputers. Over the next couple of decades, scientists and meteorologists worked together to formulate a universal model for Earth's weather patterns, gathering data across the globe from satellites. However, as it stands today, the world's best forecasts were speculative beyond two or three days, and beyond six or seven, they were worthless.

There Is No A.I.

Even with perfect sensors spaced one foot apart and an infinitely powerful computer, tiny fluctuations, smaller than the sensor grid, introduce errors in the system. These errors grow exponentially over time due to the nonlinear dynamics of the atmosphere. Even with the difference of a minute in measurement time, tiny deviations at the one-foot scale amplify and cascade to larger scales (ten feet, then miles) until they affect global weather patterns. Edward Lorenz, the pioneer who had first trodden the path of weather modelling on his Royal McBee computer, had warned about the doom of long-range weather forecasting after his harsh realization of the unpredictability of the system. (Lorenz 1979). While running simulations, he accidentally altered an input value by a mere 0.000127 (truncating from 0.506127 to 0.506). He had expected negligible deviation from the expected pattern; however, the emerging pattern was drastically different. The chaotic nature of the weather was at play. But the very prospect of getting a glimpse of the future has had many sane minds losing it in despair.

Humans have had a fascination with prediction since ancient times. Earlier, the predictions and prophecies were made based on some natural or cosmic events, such as the sighting of a rare bird or a comet. The Romans used to observe bird flight patterns to interpret divine will, which would guide them in their decisions in warfare, politics, and agriculture. History has accounts full of seers, clairvoyants, soothsayers, and fortune tellers, who used to prophesy the events of the future, especially doomsday-type events. In fact, they were quite celebrated ones. Even today, who is not familiar with the name of French apothecary Michel de Nostradamus, who published Les Prophéties (1555), a collection of quatrains predicting future events in vague, symbolic language. He kept his prophecies ambiguous, which allowed for broad interpretation and invited all sorts of imagination to be applied to his vague model.

However, with time, better sense prevailed among humans, and science started to gain recognition in society as a valid explanation of cosmic events based upon data. And this movement was pioneered by none other than Nicolaus Copernicus, who used empirical observation, mathematics, and logic to predict planetary motions, and even to demonstrate that the Earth orbited around the Sun. Works of Copernicus, documented in On the Revolutions of the Heavenly Spheres (1543), laid the groundwork for modern astronomy and scientific forecasting. (Nicolaus Copernicus 1995). Later in 1689, Lloyd's of London began using historical data on sea voyages to predict risks and set insurance premiums. By analysing past trip outcomes, they estimated the likelihood of future losses.

Back in time, predictions about lifespan were not much of a large-scale business, but insurers and statisticians in the 19th century reduced death to a mathematical probability. Although superstition in societies slowly started getting replaced by empirical data in practical decision making, modern statistical methods were developed only in the last century, which enabled systematic predictions based on numerical data, and applied in fields from economics to meteorology. Weather Forecasting, no doubt, was a very non-trivial task to begin with, and attain a fully proven model inspired the usage of computers to model complex systems. Scientists from all dimensions hoped to make predictions about the domain they were concerned with. If weather forecasting was a start, next in line was economic forecasting, and so on.

Oh wait! If probabilistic predictions have been around for centuries, or say the last century based on data, then how come A.I. models, which are nothing but probabilistic models supported by high computing devices with significant carbon emission, are game changers? Why are scientists even promoting this fallacy?

In the words of Michael Crichton, *"The ultimate lesson is that science isn't special—at least not anymore. Maybe back when Einstein talked to Niels Bohr, and there were only a few dozen important workers in every field. But there are now three million researchers in America. It's no longer a calling, it's a career. Science is as corruptible a human activity as any other. Its practitioners aren't saints, they're human beings, and they do what human beings do— lie, cheat, steal from one another, sue, hide data, fake data, overstate their own importance, and denigrate opposing views unfairly. That's human nature. It isn't going to change. (Crichton 2006)"*

But Crichton was not alone in his pessimistic yet realistic view about the new brigade of scientists in modern times. A few decades earlier, the famous historian of science, Thomas S. Kuhn, in his highly influential yet controversial book *The Structure of Scientific Revolutions (1962)* puts forward the notion that average scientists carry out only *"mopping up operations"*, which are nothing but modified versions of experiments that have been carried out many times before. In the case of Artificial Intelligence or Machine Learning, if you look at the famous algorithms in use, such as clustering or Principal Component Analysis (PCA), or even others, most are around 80-100 years old. Mathematics behind the technology has not changed much, but only gradual modifications have been made based on specific use cases or insights. Kuhn argues that today, scientists or researchers first must adopt a body of terminology and mathematical techniques before making advances in any specific field, but in return, in an unconscious way, they lose the freedom to question the foundations of the field (Gleick 1988). The scientific revolutions come up by solving puzzles that have reached dead ends, and this often unorthodox and non-linear thinking draws inspiration from fields outside the domain of the puzzle.

Story of Radio Hat

During the 1940s, radio was a popular form of entertainment, which shaped how people consume media. The portable version of it, which worked upon vacuum tubes and transistors, became quite a rage. The Merri-Lei Corporation, a lesser-known electronics firm, sought to capitalize on this trend by introducing the Radio Hat in 1949. The product was designed by Victor T. Hoey and marketed as a wearable radio, which integrated a receiver into a pith helmet-style hat and complete with antenna loops and tuning knobs. The Merri-Lei Corporation launched an aggressive marketing campaign to position the Radio Hat as a revolutionary device. Advertisements appeared in popular magazines like Life and Popular Science, which showcased young people wearing the colourful hats while engaging in fun activities like sunbathing or strolling. The Radio Hat was presented as a symbol of modernity, which promised to make radio listening a seamless part of daily life. Some ads even claimed it was "the radio sensation of the century," and celebrities were hired to promote the product.

When launched in the market, the Radio Hat garnered significant attention for its novelty; however, its impracticalities quickly became apparent. The hat was bulky, despite claims of being lightweight, and the protruding antenna loops were prone to damage. The design was also less fashionable than advertised, with the pith helmet style clashing with everyday wear. Moreover, the radio's functionality was limited to AM stations, and its sound quality was mediocre compared to standalone portable radios. Consumer feedback was not promising as well. Consumers claimed that the hat was uncomfortable for extended wear, and the battery life was short. Regulatory challenges also emerged, as some cities restricted their use in public spaces due to concerns about distracted pedestrians. In a couple of years, the Radio Hat's novelty had worn off, and it faced stiff competition from more practical portable radios, such as the Regency TR-1, the first transistor radio, released in 1954, which offered superior portability without the need for a cumbersome hat. The Merri-Lei Corporation attempted to sustain interest by offering the Radio Hat as a promotional item at gas stations and department stores, but production ceased within a few years. By the mid-1950s, the product had faded into obscurity. (Schiffer 1991).

Internet's Doom

If the Telephone was a solution for one-to-one communication, between individuals sitting distance apart, which worked on electrical signal transmission, then Radio (and later TV) was a promoter for one-to-many broadcast, which worked on radio signal transmission. And both these solutions worked on the principle of electromagnetism. And then came the Internet in the 1990s, which promoted new forms of communication (many-to-many), information sharing, and commerce. It was indeed a pivotal period of human history, which presented a prospect of the entire globe as one connected entity. This period saw the rapid proliferation of internet-based companies, dubbed "dotcoms" due to their ".com" domain names. However, instead of the technology (electromagnetism and computer systems), Dot-com companies were marketed as revolutionary, which promised to disrupt traditional industries. Traditional Commerce was now e-commerce. Pets.com was pitched as a game changer, but it was nothing but an online pet supply retailer, which faced the same logistical challenges as brick-and-mortar retailers. Webvan aimed to revolutionize grocery shopping with online ordering and home delivery, but incurred massive losses due to expensive infrastructure and low margins. However, the hype was epitomized by claims in Dow 36,000 that internet companies justified sky-high valuations due to their potential to dominate markets. Remember, any object resting idly at a place will have some potential energy. Potential energy is associated with forces that act on a body in a way that the total work done by these forces on the body depends only on the initial and final positions of the body in space. Then surely to transform a business, one would need to convert this Potential energy into some other kind of energy, say Kinetic energy. But that propellant in most of these businesses was missing.

Amazon's early success further fuelled the perception that any internet-based business was inherently revolutionary. But the ground reality was still the same. Businesses were still being done on the ground; the virtual world just enabled the efficiency of communication. But the efficiency of internet communication, which slowly became the standard way of communication, was not a guarantee for an efficient business model. Despite the hype, many dot-com ventures were traditional businesses repackaged for the internet and lacked sustainable business models. These companies relied on the internet's novelty to attract investment but failed to address core business challenges. (Cassidy 2002). The NASDAQ Composite Index, heavily weighted with tech stocks, soared from 1,000 in 1995 to over 5,000 by March 2000, driven by speculative fervour rather than sound fundamentals. And then the inevitable happened.

By early 2000, investors began questioning the sustainability of dot-com valuations. Companies like Pets.com, which spent heavily on marketing (remember its famous Super Bowl ad featuring a sock puppet?), collapsed when revenue failed to materialize. The U.S. Federal Reserve raised interest rates in 1999–2000 to curb inflation, which increases borrowing costs for unprofitable startups. As flagship dotcoms like Webvan and eToys filed for bankruptcy, investor confidence plummeted. Finally, the NASDAQ crashed, falling 78% from its peak of 5,048 in March 2000 to 1,114 by October 2002. Trillions were washed out in market value, with many dotcoms disappearing entirely. If the dotcom boom was a triumph of marketing over substance, then its crash was a required course correction by the laws of nature. But there were survivors, like Amazon, PayPal, eBay, etc., who focused on sustainable growth.

Is History repeating itself?

In the past, history has repeated itself, but is history again repeating itself? Answering the question itself is paradoxical, as we have learnt already that connecting the dots in the past for a dynamic system is easier than predicting the future, where a small change in input or initial conditions can lead to a drastic change in outcome. In the chaos theory, this is also called *the butterfly effect*. Then what do we learn from history? One must learn to evaluate objectively.

These are still very early days for the so-called A.I. models, which are nothing but machine learning models boosted by high computational availability, which come at a cost. Like the internet, it is also nothing more than a tool, which, if used effectively, can improve the efficiency of the business. But again, the key to success is effective business strategy, not the tool itself. And with respect to the efficiency of the tool and its touted potential to replace human intelligence, we have had enough discussion in past chapters. Then, one must question why the big tech giants and media are signalling the end of human labour, directly or indirectly.

Historically, humans have been driven by herd behaviour. After all, we are animals! After Apple's iPhone launch in 2007, competitors like Samsung and Nokia scrambled to release touch-screen smartphones. Considering feature phones obsolete, consumers rushed to buy them by paying a premium price. Even though early smartphones had clunky interfaces or limited apps, herd behavior, fueled by Apple's marketing and media hype, drove mass adoption of smartphones. But if you take a note, even today, just 6 months after the launch, the price of an existing model of a smartphone drops alarmingly, especially if timed with a new release with some minor tweaks and proper marketing gimmicks. Imagine buying a phone at Rs. 1,00,000 in May, but only to find out that within six months of the launch, the value of the so-called 'premium' product you own is now reduced by 30% and is being sold at Rs. 70,000. This story plays out every time, and a herd of consumers gets lured all the time. In the case of the so-called A.I. revolution as well, big players are creating a bandwagon effect by showcasing AI's transformative potential in ads, keynotes, and whitepapers. For example, Microsoft's Copilot integration across Office tools or Amazon's AI-driven logistics optimizations signal that AI is the standard. Businesses adopt AI to stay competitive, and consumers buy AI-enabled products to feel cutting-edge, even if the added value is marginal. The proliferation of AI chatbots in customer service is a case study in itself. Many companies deploy AI chatbots not because they outperform human agents but because competitors are doing it. Consumers encounter these bots in every app or website, even when it frustrates them, all thanks to endless loops of unhelpful responses.

If you look closely, it is planned obsolescence at play. Companies use software updates, feature exclusivity, or cultural messaging to make past products seem inferior, and it eventually drives continuous consumption from the customers. If you do not believe me, check YouTube videos for the long queues of people sleeping outside Apple Stores across the world, just to hold a new model. Ironically, these manipulated customers are ready to pay the premium price to sleep on the streets for products which is nothing but a mere upgrade marketed as the next big thing, and then there are people on the streets who do not have a blanket to cover themselves in the cold. As Chaplin says, *"Life is a tragedy when seen in close-up, but a comedy in long-shot"*.

Sadly, in the case of A.I., the game of obsolescence has transcended the boundary. It is no more the products which are getting obsolete but the consumers itself on whose data these tech giants have built these models (*and ethics and legality of data collection part remains questionable*), as A.I. promoters are projecting to replace human talent with these 'intelligent' machines and claim to even lower the cost. And all it takes is some casual statement here and there, backed by unsubstantial data, and promoted by media on the loop, which creates a butterfly effect in the masses and sends them into a frenzy. A single AI breakthrough or viral claim about automation can reshape hiring practices, investor priorities, and worker anxieties, which in turn creates a ripple effect that exaggerates AI's impact. As the trends are currently in 2025, every now and then, a CEO comes out and prophesies on lines like "AI will replace 80% of developers". These events spark media coverage, corporate adoption of AI tools, and reduced hiring for entry-level coders, as companies chase the "AI revolution". AI tools like Copilot X or JetBrains' AI Assistant are widely adopted these days, with claims that they can "code faster than humans". Yet, these tools often produce generic or insecure code for complex projects, which ultimately requires human intervention. But again, these trends and events are not new but have been repeated in the past.

A century earlier, the process of weaving fabric was a labour-intensive task carried out by skilled weavers using hand looms. Each step of the process, from setting up the warp to manipulating the shuttle, required careful manual work. With inventions like the Jacquard loom, the speed and efficiency of the weaving process significantly improved. While it did displace some traditional hand weavers, it also led to the creation of new job opportunities in machine operation, maintenance, and design. History is full of such examples. When Henry Ford introduced assembly lines for car manufacturing, it revolutionized the automobile industry by significantly increasing production efficiency, reducing the time and effort required for each task. Computers have been automating tasks for us humans right from their advent. Word processing, spreadsheet software, and email systems streamlined administrative processes, allowing workers to focus on more complex cognitive tasks. Nowadays, Robots are employed in tasks such as welding, painting, and assembly, freeing human workers from repetitive and physically demanding activities. Even the field of agriculture has been adopting technology throughout the course of human history. The usage of tractors and harvesters has automated many farming tasks, which has helped farmers to shift focus on better crop management and decision making.

Technology has always been a disruptive force and has challenged established order and processes. However, as new technologies are integrated and adapted, a new order emerges (remember dissipative structures? Refer to chapter 2). This new order often brings increased efficiency, convenience, and improvements in various aspects of life. From the invention of the wheel to the development of the internet, each technological leap has contributed to reducing entropy in the way we live and work. For example, advances in transportation technology, from trains to airplanes, have reduced the entropy of geographical barriers. What was once a cumbersome and time-consuming journey has become more efficient, connecting people and cultures across the globe. Vaccines, antibiotics, and medical technologies have contributed to longer and healthier lives, reducing uncertainty in the face of diseases.

The Plot

In 2022, Klarna, a Swedish fintech company known for its *"buy now, pay later services*, laid off around 700 employees and embraced AI-powered systems, primarily through a partnership with OpenAI. By 2023, this fintech giant had halted the recruitment of human workers and relied heavily on generative AI for tasks such as translation, data analysis, and even art production. Klarna CEO, Sebastian Siemiatkowski, claimed publicly in 2023 that "*AI can already do all of the jobs that we, as humans, do*".

And hardly a year has passed since the proclamation, Klarna is now dealing with inefficiencies of A.I. systems, and plans to hire back humans in the loop through a large-scale recruitment drive. In his own words to Bloomberg, Siemiatkowski confesses, "*Cost unfortunately seems to have been a too predominant evaluation factor when organising this, what you end up having is lower quality*". He further clarifies, "*From a brand perspective, a company perspective, I just think it's so critical that you are clear to your customer that there will always be a human if you want*". He does not stop at this, though. He even plans to bring back 'not so intelligent humans' by offering their customer service as a 'VIP thing' (Davis 2025). But Klarna is not alone in this; most importantly, they have openly acknowledged their shortsightedness. On the contrary, there are big tech CEOs who are just trying to confuse the common human beings by mixing in arbitrary terms to keep the topic relevant and hide their short-sightedness. Recently, Mr Sundar Pichai, Google CEO, suggested a new term for their models, which are prone to hallucinating, misinformation, and simple errors, and placed them under "artificial jagged intelligence (AJI)", which is just a point of passing in the pursuit of "artificial general intelligence". Pichai chose to build upon the narrative set by Andrej Karpathy, who reportedly confessed about the roadblocks of current A.I. models that *"the issue is that unlike humans, "where a lot of knowledge and problem-solving capabilities are all highly correlated and improve linearly all together, from birth to adulthood," the jagged edges of AI are not always clear or predictable"*. Pichai, being out of the character, projects his understanding of the situation not based upon data or any insights but 'feelings' that *"I feel like we are in the AJI phase where dramatic progress, some things don't work well, but overall, you're seeing lots of progress"* (Varanasi 2025).

The very idea of presenting a model having "General Intelligence" is also concerning. If you are an old timer and have a thing for sayings, you may recall *"Jack of all trades, master of none"*. Look at the present-day schooling system. Children in middle school are encouraged to participate in "extracurricular activities," and in high school, they compete even harder to appear omnicompetent. By the time they get to college, students have already spent a decade of their academic career curating a bewilderingly diverse resume to prepare for a completely unknowable future. And honestly, they are not ready for anything. (Thiel 2014).

Howard Gardner, a renowned psychologist, pressed forward the idea of multiple intelligences in his seminal book *"Frames of Mind"*. He categorically calls out the idea of a single unified view of intelligence in humans (often equated with IQ) as overly narrow, empirically limited, and biased. In his words, *"Reason, intelligence, logic, and knowledge are not synonymous"*. The tech giants promoting this idea of an Artificial General Intelligence, which can overshadow the capacities of human intelligence, seem sinister as it celebrates certain traits, such as logical reasoning or linguistic capabilities, but downgrades other human abilities, such as musical, spatial, or bodily-kinesthetic capacities. Humans show signs of multiple intelligences present in them. For example, damage to Broca's area in the brain may impair linguistic intelligence without affecting musical or spatial abilities, which contradicts the notion of a single, general intelligence. However, this view of adhering to a general intelligence system is not new and has already led to educational systems that prioritize a narrow set of skills, disadvantaging students with strengths in other areas. These are nothing but signs of a society governed by authoritarian leaders who aim to radically transform their societies according to a specific ideological or political agenda. Their underlying aim is to seek total control over societal structures, often suppressing dissent to enforce a unified vision. And it has often been done historically by alienating entities associated with reason, critical thinking, and intellectual inquiry.

And if one carefully looks at the ecosystems being created by tech giants like Google or Microsoft, parallels can be drawn immediately. Their expansive visions are often plots to shape societal interactions through technology, leveraging their platforms to influence behavior, information flow, and economic systems. A 2020 New York Times article notes that lawmakers accused Google, Amazon, Facebook, and Apple of serving as "gatekeepers" that make third-party businesses beholden to their demands, with the term "monopoly" appearing nearly 120 times in a congressional report. (June 2020). Quest to monopoly is not a bad thing, as Peter Thiel suggests, it is the condition of every successful business. In an ideal yet dynamic world, creative monopolists give customers more choices by adding entirely new categories of abundance to the world. But the line between *'choice'* and *'control'* is getting blurred day by day in the new ecosystem that is at play. Nevertheless, the aim of this book is not to go too far into the intent of the totalitarian regimes but to focus on the capabilities and potential of the so-called *"Intelligent"* models.

The rumours of widespread dissatisfaction from A.I. integrations are now floating in the air, but somehow not given enough voice by the biased media, dancing on the whims of capitalists. If the play here by the capitalists is to reduce the human value by demeaning their self-worth and making them doubt their ability, then this is not going to play out very well for either side.

For instance, let us consider a possible scenario where a newly released AI model can generate videos of much better quality with vivid details, based on prompts only. What can be the possible effects of this development? The video editors are no longer required. To some extent, cinematographers are also affected. You just type in prompts, and AI brings forward real-looking faces imitating Al Pacino and delivering dialogues. This even makes the actors expandable, at least the supporting cast, if we are to be generous in our assumptions. Songs and scores are, anyway, being composed by A.I. models at the time of writing this book. In short, we get a movie with minimal human involvement at the budget of prompt inference of AI models and some additional costs, which cannot be neglected.

But who will be watching or consuming such products? Humans connect via emotions. Cinema is an experience that brings people together across the globe, and everybody judges the story from their perspective. A product without humans involved will not be able to convey emotions, no matter how many vivid details A.I. can capture frame by frame. After all, *eyes don't lie*!

Thanks to braver artists like Tom Cruise, who made a movie against A.I. in 2025 (Mission Impossible), on a much grander scale and performed the deadliest stunts himself, to elevate human experience. When the audience knows that there is an actual human risking his life out there to entertain them, they are immediately hooked and appreciate the effort. They feel connected to the story and the emotion behind it. But if they realize that it is all staged and animated by A.I. models, they do not feel any connection. Recently, Marvel (backed by Disney) has faced significant backlash for using excessive CGI in their movies, resulting in a loss of the human touch. Their films have struggled since the release of Avengers: Endgame. Kevin Feige, who leads the Marvel Cinematic Universe, has reportedly brought stakeholders to the drawing board, and together they are exploring ideas to make their movies and TV shows with audiences like before.

And this is not just about cinema. It affects all parts of life. We already discussed earlier why A.I. writing feels so bland, and almost always, one can make out whether a certain text has been written by an A.I. model or a human. Now, consider the experience you get in a family dinner where food is now being prepared by AI-powered robots. When we cook with our hands, we cook with certain emotions. They reflect in the taste of the food being prepared. Ever noticed, when mother is not in her jovial mood, the spices proportion is on the higher side, or breads are a bit burnt. When she prepares for her kid's birthday, she pours in all her emotions, and that is what makes the food so delicious that we crave it from time to time. It evokes certain memories, even the aroma of cooking is enough to do that. And it stands true even for the chefs in a restaurant. We all have our favourite places for hangout, where we go only to relish certain delicacies, the experience of which we think cannot be replaced. Be it *panipuri* in India or pizza in Italy, emotions with food stay the same. Good luck having such experience with trained Robots.

And what would be the economic consequence?

A product produced by AI to be further consumed by A.I.?

By pitching the supremacy of A.I. models, tech giants are trying to project an indefinitely optimistic world where they claim the future to be better than the present, but they do not showcase any specific plans to do it. The future is expected to yield profit, but there are no designs for it. Investments are not being made to build a new product, but already developed products are being rearranged. For instance, most of the research in biotech startups is hinged on random probabilistic experiments rather than refinement of definite theories about how the body's systems operate. And despite all the recent advancements in technology which aid this kind of research, the number of new drugs approved per billion dollars spent on R&D has halved every nine years since 1950 (Eroom's Law).

For a moment, if we buy into the hype of A.I., then we must analyse its pitfalls. With the supposed productivity gains from A.I., the cost of producing labour-intensive tasks will fall. In a competitive market, these tasks are now cheaper to produce and thus more abundant. However, this does not guarantee a reduction in demand for other tasks. The prices for these now-abundant tasks fall sharply to an extent that the price decline is greater than the initial gain in physical productivity. Even if this technology leads to a small wage increase, the overall value of what labour produces (relative to capital) goes down. (Acemoglu 2024). And with more productivity in less effort, there will be layoffs. Unless these workers, who are not needed for the tasks already automated, find other tasks to do or new tasks are created for them, they may face lower wages or unemployment. The cost savings from automation raise the net productivity, but unless the economy reinvests those savings into job-creating sectors, displaced workers do not benefit. (Acemoglu 2024). The world leaders may flash rising GDPs, but wages will stagnate or decline for low and mid-skill roles. This will only end up increasing the income gap between labourers and capital owners. Peter Thiel sums it up: *"At no point does anyone in the chain know about what to do with money in the real economy."* It has become human nature in general to prefer unlimited optionality where money is more valuable than anything, and we have no idea how to create wealth.

In life, nothing comes free, and with mass lay-offs, who would be consuming entertainment at a price? And if products are not being bought in the market, what would supply the funds necessary for future products? After all, A.I. models do have some infrastructure cost, and they are costly. Even the tech giants will require significant investment to support the digital infrastructure based on the projected demand of the growth of their user base. And even if somehow all the costs are covered, will we still be living in an independent setup? Imagine the plight of an economically weaker country that is dependent on digital infrastructures and AI-powered systems over which it has no control at all? Are we promoting a world of data colonies where humans are traded for data? Long-term planning is often undervalued in this indefinitely optimistic short-term world. (Thiel 2014).

The race to acquire information and use it to manipulate the world in the name of acquiring *intelligence* does not seem so *intelligent* after all. It is not the intelligence they are after, but money and power. And data is the key to unlock this power of unlimited potential. There are many dimensions to this idea. We have already discussed how companies track the behavioral traits of their consumers to feed them ideas or suggestions of products they are most likely to accept, and thus end up creating echo chambers. It would be naïve to think that the role of social media in the Myanmar turmoil was a one-off incident. Different nations are now facing unique challenges when it comes to managing information and misinformation. It is now much easier to gather people for rallies and protests. All you have to feed them is a certain narrative, almost like a time bomb being prepared to explode.

One of the most significant inventions of the 20th century, the internet, which was meant to bring people closer to each other, may potentially be used by hidden players to split the end users into segregated information cocoons, each driven by their own perceived reality. And one should not count out the smaller players for long, as people across the globe have already started seeing through the picture, and it will bring out more independent players onto the stage, and the world is then going to be ever more chaotic. Ironically, that is the whole point of the second law of thermodynamics. In all jest, the story of Victor Frankenstein creating a sapient creature, who, once being rejected by humanity, seeks revenge from the creator itself, has already been prophesied.

End Note

Humans are social creatures, at least for the foreseeable future! Most of our decision-making is based on the social connections we form and the society we live in. Yes, as a customer, we like prompt responses to our queries, but when it comes to closing a deal, we would like to know who is sitting behind the screen. Who are we going to blame or hold accountable if things go wrong? Trust plays a crucial role in decision-making. Knowing the individuals behind a product or service creates a sense of trust and reliability. People are more likely to engage in transactions when there is a perceived connection with the individuals or entities involved. And this connection can be enhanced with a better experience, and this is where the confluence of AI and humans lies. From recommending products to tailoring marketing messages, AI can help deliver a more personalized and satisfying customer experience, but only if human experience is kept alive. No one likes to make love with a dead doll, and such an act only fosters the death of civilization.

There is always going to be a symbiotic relationship between humans and technology. It is all about how cognizant we are in making use of technology. Till the time human emotions and social connections are the driving force of society, we must not fear technological advancements, as they will be the tools to bring order to the chaos. The dystopian future of machines taking over humans can remain fiction!

There Is No A.I.

References

Acemoglu, Daron. "The Simple Macroeconomics of AI." Massachusetts Institute of Technology, 5 April 2024.

al, Dale Purves et. *Neuroscience.* Sunderland, Massachusetts U.S.A.: Sinauer Associates, Inc, 2018.

Aristotle, translated by W.D. Ross. *Metaphysics, Book IV.* Oxford University Press, 1924.

Ashish Vaswani, Noam Shazeer, Niki Parmar, Jakob Uszkoreit, Llion Jones, Aidan N. Gomez, Lukasz Kaiser, Illia Polosukhin. "Attention Is All You Need." 2017.

Attwell, D., & Laughlin, S. B. "An energy budget for signaling in the grey matter of the brain." *Journal of Cerebral Blood Flow & Metabolism,* 2001.

Bender, E. M., Gebru, T., McMillan-Major, A., & Shmitchell, S. "On the Dangers of Stochastic Parrots: Can Language Models Be Too Big? ." *Proceedings of the 2021 ACM Conference on Fairness, Accountability, and Transparency,* 2021.

Bobzien, Susanne. "Stoic Logic." *The Cambridge Companion to the Stoics, Cambridge University Press,* 2003.

Bonner, Anthony. *The Art and Logic of Ramon Llull: A User's Guide.* Leiden: Brill, 2007.

Buzsáki, G., Anastassiou, C. A., & Koch, C. "The origin of extracellular fields and currents—EEG, ECoG, LFP and spikes." *Nature Reviews Neuroscience, 13(6), 407–420*, 2012.

Buzsaki, Gyorgy. *Rhythms of the Brain*. Oxford University Press, 2006.

Cassidy, John. *Dot.con: The Greatest Story Ever Sold*. HarperCollins, 2002.

Chakrabarti, K. K. *Classical Indian Philosophy of Mind: The Nyāya Dualist Tradition*. SUNY Press, 1999.

Cho, K., van Merriënboer, B., Gulcehre, C., Bahdanau, D., Bougares, F., Schwenk, H., & Bengio, Y. (2014). "Learning phrase representations using RNN encoder-decoder for statistical machine translation." *Proceedings of the 2014 Conference on Empirical Methods in Natural Language Processing (EMNLP), 1724–1734. DOI: 10.3115/v1/D14-1179*, n.d.

Coldewey, Devin. *https://techcrunch.com/*. 24 July 2024. https://techcrunch.com/2024/07/24/model-collapse-scientists-warn-against-letting-ai-eat-its-own-tail/.

Crichton, Michael. *Next*. HarperCollins, 2006.

Curd, P. "Presocratic Philosophy." In *Stanford Encyclopedia of Philosophy*. 2019.

D H HUBEL, T N WIESEL. "Receptive fields, binocular interaction and functional architecture in the cat's visual cortex." *Journal of Physiology*, 1962.

Davis, Dominic-Madori. "Klarna CEO says company will use humans to offer VIP customer service." *TechCrunch.* 4 June 2025. https://techcrunch.com/2025/06/04/klarna-ceo-says-company-will-use-humans-to-offer-vip-customer-service/.

Dayan, P. and Abbott, L.F. *Theoretical Neuroscience: Computational and Mathematical Modeling of Neural Systems.* Cambridge: The MIT Press, 2001.

Diogenes Laertius, translated by R.D. Hicks. *Lives of Eminent Philosophers, Book VII.* Loeb Classical Library, 1925.

Eichenbaum, H., Cohen, N. J. (2001). "From conditioning to conscious recollection: Memory systems of the brain." 2001.

Gigerenzer, G. *Rationality for Mortals: How People Cope with Uncertainty.* Oxford University Press, 2008.

Gleick, James. *Chaos: Making a New Science.* Penguin, 1988.

Greene, Tristan. *AI benchmarking scandal: Were top models caught gaming the system?* The Stack. 13 January 2025. https://www.thestack.technology/ai-benchmarking-scandal-were-top-models-caught-gaming-the-system/.

Hameroff, S., & Penrose, R. "Consciousness in the Universe: A Review of the 'Orch OR' Theory." *Physics of Life Reviews,* 2014.

Harari, Yuval Noah. *Nexus: A BRIEF HISTORY OF INFORMATION NETWORKS*. New York: Random House, n.d.

Hochreiter, S., & Schmidhuber, J. (1997). "Long short-term memory." *Neural Computation 9(8), 1735–1780. DOI: 10.1162/neco.1997.9.8.1735*, n.d.

Hodgkin, A. L., & Huxley, A. F. (1952a). "Currents carried by sodium and potassium ions through the membrane of the giant axon of Loligo." *Journal of Physiology, 116(4), 449–472*, n.d.

Ilia Shumailov, Zakhar Shumaylov, Yiren Zhao, Nicolas Papernot, Ross Anderson & Yarin Gal. "AI models collapse when trained on recursively generated data." *Nature* 631 (2024): 755–759.

Izhikevich, E. M. *Dynamical Systems in Neuroscience: The Geometry of Excitability and Bursting*. MIT Press, 2007.

John E Lisman, Ole Jensen. "The Theta-Gamma Neural Code." 2013.

Josselyn, S. A., & Tonegawa. "Memory engrams: Recalling the past and imagining the future." *Science, 367(6473), eaaw4325*, n.d.

Juliet Bockhorst, Abraham Brownell, Paloma Noriega Burrill, Catherine Crossin, Leo Crossman, Logan Douglas, Nick Antonellis, Robin Kass, Sasha Cadariu, Wuyue Zhou. *Computational Neuroscience*. licensed under CC BY-SA 4.0, n.d.

June, Daisuke WakabayashiMike IsaacKaren WeiseJack Nicas and Sophia. "13 Ways the Government Went After Google, Facebook and Other Tech Giants This Year." *The New York Times.* 2020. https://www.nytimes.com/interactive/2020/technology/tech-investigations.html.

Kerferd, G. B. *The Sophistic Movement.* Cambridge: Cambridge University Press, 1981.

Laurenza, Domenico. *Leonardo's Machines: Da Vinci's Inventions Revealed.* Florence: Giunti, 2006.

Lennie, P. "The cost of cortical computation." *Current Biology,* 2003.

Liao, Q., Wang, Y., Zhang, Z. "The Limits of Benchmark-Driven AI Development." *arXiv* , no. arXiv:2402.12345 (n.d.).

Lorenz, Edward. "On the prevalence of aperiodicity in simple systems." 1979.

Machiavelli, N. , Translated by W.K. Marriott. *The Prince.* 1908.

Marc W Howard, Daniel S Rizzuto, Jeremy B Caplan, Joseph R Madsen, John Lisman, Richard Aschenbrenner-Scheibe, Andreas Schulze-Bonhage, Michael J Kahana. "Gamma oscillations correlate with working memory load in humans." 2001.

Matheus Henrique Ferreira, Patricia Renovato Tobo,Carla Regina Barrichello,Mirella Gualtieri. "Olfactory interference on the emotional processing speed of visual stimuli: The influence of facial expressions intensities." *PLOS One*, no. e0264261 - May 2022 (2022).

Minsky, M., & Papert, S. (1969). "Perceptrons: An introduction to computational geometry." *MIT Press*, n.d.

Nicolaus Copernicus, trans. C. G. Wallis. *On the Revolutions of the Heavenly Spheres*. Prometheus Books, 1995.

Pariser, E. *The Filter Bubble: What the Internet Is Hiding from You*. Pengion Press, 2011.

Patterson, D., et al. "Carbon emissions and large neural network training." *arXiv preprint arXiv:2104.10350*, 2021.

Penrose, Roger. *The Emperor's New Mind*. OUP Oxford, 1989.

Pitts, W. S. McCulloch and W. "A logical calculus of the ideas immanent in nervous activity." *The bulletin of mathematical biophysics* 5 (1943).

Rapoport, A. Shimbel and A. "A statistical approach to the theory of the central nervous system." *The Bulletin of Mathematical Biophysics* 10 (1948): 41–55.

Rosenblatt, F. (1958). "The perceptron: A probabilistic model for information storage and organization in the brain." *Psychological Review, 65(6), 386–408. DOI: 10.1037/h0042519*, n.d.

Schiffer, M. B. *The Portable Radio in American Life.* University of Arizona Press, 1991.

Schwiening, C. J. "A brief historical perspective: Hodgkin and Huxley." *Journal of Physiology, 590(11), 2571–2575*, 2012.

Sedley, David. "Hellenistic Philosophy and Science." *The Cambridge History of Hellenistic Philosophy, Cambridge University Press* (Cambridge University Press), 1999.

Shanahan, M. "Talking About Large Language Models." *Communications of the ACM,67(2), 68–79.*, 2024.

Stanislas Dehaene, Manuela Piazza, Philippe Pinel, Laurent Cohen. "Three parietal circuits for number processing." 2003.

Strubell, E., et al. "Energy and policy considerations for deep learning in NLP." *Proceedings of the 57th Annual Meeting of the Association for Computational Linguistics*, 2019.

Stuart Russell, Peter Norvig. *Artificial Intelligence, A Modern Approach.* n.d.

T V Bliss, G L Collingridge. "A synaptic model of memory: long-term potentiation in the hippocampus." *Nature. 1993 Jan 7;361(6407):31-9. doi: 10.1038/361031a0. PMID: 8421494.*, 1993.

The Brain from Top to Bottom. n.d. https://thebrain.mcgill.ca/.

Thiel, Peter. *Zero To One.* Penguin Random House, 2014.

Thomas Aquinas, translated by Richard Berquist. *Commentary on Aristotle's Posterior Analytics.* Notre Dame: Dumb Ox Books, 2007.

Tony Street, edited by Khaled El-Rouayheb and Sabine Schmidtke. "Avicenna and the Development of Logic." In *The Oxford Handbook of Islamic Philosophy.* Oxford University Press, 2016.

Travis John Adrian Craddock, Douglas Friesen, Jonathan Mane, Stuart Hameroff, Jack A Tuszynski. "The feasibility of coherent energy transfer in microtubules." *Journal of the Royal Society Interface,* 2016.

Varanasi, Lakshmi. "AI leaders have a new term for the fact that their models are not always so intelligent." *Business Insider.* 8 June 2025. https://www.businessinsider.com/aji-artificial-jagged-intelligence-google-ceo-sundar-pichai-2025-6?token=eyJhbGciOiJIUzI1NiIsInR5cCI6IkpXVCJ9.eyJmaXJzdF9uYW1lIjoiUmVlc2hhYmgiLCJsYXNoX25hbWUiOiJDaG91ZGhhcnkiLCJtZW1iZXJfaWQiOiJmNTdlMTk3OC00YWQ2LTRiMTEtOTU4M.

Vidyabhusana, S.C. *The Nyāya Sūtras of Gotama.* New Delhi: Motilal Banarasidass, 1990.

Warofka, Alex. *An Independent Assessment of the Human Rights Impact of Facebook in Myanmar.* Meta. 5 November 2018.

https://about.fb.com/news/2018/11/myanmar-hria/.

Werbos, P. J. (1990). " Backpropagation through time: What it does and how to do it." *Proceedings of the IEEE, 78(10), 1550–1560. DOI: 10.1109/5.58337*, n.d.

William E. Boyce, Richard C. DiPrima. *Elementry Differential Equations and Boundary value problems*. John Wiley & Sons, Inc., 2005.

William Kneale, Martha Kneale. *The Development of Logic*. Oxford: Clarendon Press, 1962.

Williams, Michael R. *A History of Computing Technology*. Englewood Cliffs: Prentice-Hall, 1985.

Zaleznik, Daniel. "Facebook and Genocide: How Facebook contributed to genocide in Myanmar and why it will not be held accountable." *Home* 1 (n.d.).

There Is No A.I.

www.ingramcontent.com/pod-product-compliance
Lightning Source LLC
Chambersburg PA
CBHW041317120726
48005CB00014B/2028